THE OFFICIAL **NATIONAL PARK GUIDE**

NORTH YORK MOORS

Text by Ian Sampson · Photographs by Ian Carstairs

SERIES EDITOR **Roly Smith**

PEVENSEY GUIDES

The Pevensey Press is an imprint of
David & Charles

First published in the UK in 2001

Map artwork by Chartwell Illustrators
based on material supplied by the
North York Moors National Park
Authority

Text copyright © Ian Sampson 2001
Photographs copyright © Ian
Carstairs 2001

A catalogue record for this book is
available from the British Library.

ISBN 1 898630 16 X

Book design by Les Dominey Design
Company, Exeter

Printed in Hong Kong by
Hong Kong Graphics and
Printing Ltd
for David & Charles
Brunel House Newton Abbot Devon

Contents

Page 1: Boundary stone on Blakey Ridge — the heather moorland is a man-made landscape created for sheep and grouse. Management by the landowners is essential to the continuation of the heather. The boundary between adjoining estates is sometimes marked by a stone such as here on the moor above Rosedale
Pages 2-3: Looking west from Castleton into Westerdale — a typical moorland dale with grass fields, stone walls, scattered farmsteads, shelterbelts of trees and patches of bracken — surrounded by the heather moorland
Pages 4-5: Hole of Horcum — legend suggests that the vast hollow was created by the local giant, Wade, who grasped a handful of earth to throw at his wife. In reality, it has been formed by springs 'sapping' or dissolving away the rock strata
Front cover: (above) Castleton; (below) Staithes from Cow Bar
Front flap: (left) cottage garden at Ryedale Folk Museum; (right) an ancient anchor at Whitby
Back cover: The Bridestones — the 'Ronald Reagan' stone

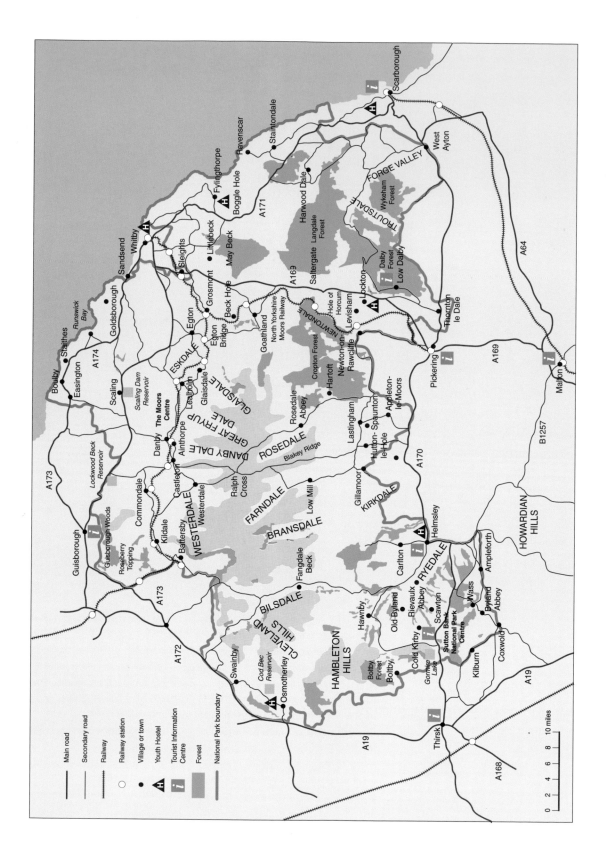

Main road

Secondary road

Railway

Railway station

Village or town

Youth Hostel

Tourist Information
Centre

Forest

National Park boundary

0   2   4   6   8   10 miles

Foreword

by Professor Ian Mercer CBE, Secretary General, Association of National Park Authorities

The National Parks of Great Britain are very special places. Their landscapes include the most remote and dramatic hills and coasts in England and Wales, as well as the wild wetlands of the Broads. They still support the farming communities which have fashioned their detail over the centuries. They form the highest rank of the protected areas which society put in place in 1949. So, 1999 saw the fiftieth anniversary of the founding legislation which, incidentally, provided for Areas of Outstanding Natural Beauty, Nature Reserves, Areas of Special Scientific Interest and Long Distance Footpaths, as well as for National Parks.

In the eight years following that, ten Parks were designated. The Lake District, the Peak, Snowdonia and Dartmoor were already well visited, as were the North York Moors, Pembrokeshire Coast, Yorkshire Dales and Exmoor which quickly followed. The Brecon Beacons and Northumberland had their devotees too, though perhaps in lesser numbers then. The special quality of each of these places was already well known, and while those involved may not have predicted the numbers, mobility or aspirations of visitors accurately, the foresight of the landscape protection system cannot be too highly praised.

That system has had to evolve – not just to accommodate visitor numbers, but to meet the pressures flowing from agricultural change, hunger for housing and roadstone, thirst for water, and military manoeuvring – and indeed, the Norfolk and Suffolk Broads were added to the list in 1989. National Parks are now cared for by freestanding authorities who control development, hold land, grant-aid farmers and others, provide wardens, information, car parks and loos, clear footpaths and litter, plant trees and partner many other agents in pursuit of the purposes for which National Parks exist. Those purposes are paramount for all public agencies' consideration when they act within the Parks. They are:

- the conservation of the natural beauty, wildlife and cultural heritage of the area, and
- the promotion of the understanding and enjoyment of its special qualities by the public.

The National Park Authorities must, in pursuing those purposes, foster social and economic well-being. They now bring in some £48 million a year between them to be deployed in the Parks, in addition to normal local public spending.

This book is first a celebration of the National Park, of all its special qualities and of the people whose predecessors produced and maintained the detail of its character. The series to which this book belongs celebrates too the first fifty years of National Park protection in the United Kingdom, the foresight of the founding fathers, and the contributions since of individuals like John Sandford, Reg Hookway and Ron Edwards. The book and the series also mark the work of the present National Park Authorities and their staff, at the beginning of the next fifty years, and of the third millennium of historic time. Their dedication to their Parks is only matched by their aspiration for the sustainable enhancement of the living landscapes for which they are responsible. They need, and hope for, your support.

In the new century, national assets will only be properly maintained if the national will to conserve them is made manifest to national governments. I hope this book will whet your appetite for the National Park, or help you get more from your visit, and provoke you to use your democratic influence on its behalf. In any case it will remind you of the glories of one of the jewels in Britain's landscape crown. Do enjoy it.

Introducing the
North York Moors

No vision of Yorkshire would ever be complete without the freedom, wildness and romance of its moors. The association between Yorkshire and its dark tracts of moorland is familiar to most. It is a link that has been nurtured and celebrated by writers throughout the nineteenth and twentieth centuries. Its most notable promoters have been the Brontë sisters, who lived in a West Yorkshire parsonage, and James Herriot whose exploits made him the world's best-known veterinary surgeon.

It also makes good television. Emotions are stirred when the scenery of a Yorkshire moor appears as a background to a television drama. This seemingly remote landscape has become world famous thanks to two major television series – 'All Creatures Great and Small' and 'Heartbeat'. For some people, arriving from all corners of the globe, Yorkshire is a place of pilgrimage. For most of us it is quite simply a beautiful area of countryside.

At the eastern side of Yorkshire is an isolated upland area whose distinctive character lies in the strength and beauty of its moors. This is the North York Moors. The name is appropriate and it holds the distinction of having the largest continuous tract of unenclosed, heather-covered moorland in England and Wales. A series of high moors, divided and separated by narrow dales, form the heartland of the area.

The high ground is gentle in relief and reaches an average of just 1,200ft (366m). Rolling moorlands with almost flat tops disappear into a horizon where the sky seems all-consuming. In Yorkshire, the area is often referred to quite simply as 'the Moors' or 'the Yorkshire Moors'.

Heather moorland covers 35 per cent of the North York Moors National Park. Nevertheless, the North York Moors did not become a National Park just because of its heather moorland. As stated in the 1947 Hobhouse Report, it contains 'within a relatively small compass an amazing wealth and variety of beauty'. Among its range of landscapes are pastoral farmland, deciduous woodlands, conifer forests and a wonderfully scenic coastline. Rugged cliffs rise out of the North Sea and the National Park has an impressive stretch of rocky coastline. With such a varied landscape and the added attraction of its many villages and historic buildings, the National Park has

Page 8: Farndale from Blakey Ridge – motorists who journey along the moorland road from Hutton le Hole to Castleton will catch glimpses of the green fields of Farndale
Page 9: A few villages in the North York Moors still have cottages with a thatched roof, such as here at Rievaulx

become a magnet for outdoor recreation and for visitors who simply come to enjoy the view.

The North York Moors was designated as a National Park in 1952. This is the highest designation given by Parliament for the protection of our countryside. The responsibilities for this Park remain with a single authority – the North York Moors National Park Authority – which is based in Helmsley. The prime responsibilities given to the National Park Authority are the protection of natural beauty, wildlife, cultural heritage and public access. These features are guarded for the benefit and enjoyment of the whole nation.

A glance at a map showing the relief of northern England will reveal that the North York Moors is a compact area, easily defined by its physical boundaries. There is lowland on three sides and the North Sea on the fourth. It stands relatively aloof from the horseshoe of surrounding lowland. Until the middle of the twentieth century, it was this relative remoteness that cushioned it from the many changes and advancements of the modern age.

Life does exist on the high moors. Humans are very thin on the ground, but one farmland animal and one bird are an unmistakable and essential part of the moorland scene. The moors are home for twelve months of the year to the moor sheep and the red grouse. A rotation of heather burning keeps the moorlands in a suitable condition for sheep grazing and grouse. For the farmers and gamekeepers involved, the financial returns from sheep and grouse are essential to their livelihood.

As an area for wildlife, the heather moorland is officially recognised as being of international importance. The vegetation suits many species of upland birds and the moors have internationally important populations of merlin and golden plover, and other birds also rely on the moorland habitat. Each springtime a fresh influx of migrant birds arrive to nest. There is nothing more evocative of the loneliness of the moors than the first plaintive and soft bubbling calls of the curlew as they seek their moorland nesting sites.

Away from the central moorland there are three principle hill ranges, all of which lie along the edges of the park. These are the Cleveland Hills, the Hambleton Hills and the Tabular Hills.

On the western boundary, running northwards from Osmotherley, are the impressive whalebacks of the Cleveland Hills. They have always presented an obstacle to access by road and rail from the west. Rising abruptly from the flat agricultural lands of the Vale of Mowbray, the line of bold sandstone hills is a major landscape feature.

South of Osmotherley are the Hambleton Hills. The underlying rocks are of limestone and the gentle relief reflects the relatively level layers of the rocks beneath. Here, the steep west-facing escarpment continues, and around Sutton Bank the rocks are exposed to view. To climb Sutton Bank, motorists must negotiate notoriously steep, hairpin bends. At the top there is the reward of a panoramic view across the vale to the Yorkshire Dales. Yorkshire's famous vet, James Herriot, claimed this to be 'the finest view in England'.

Opposite above: The continuation of steep cliffs along the coastline at Saltwick Bay provides dramatic scenery and there is little chance of direct access to the shoreline

Opposite below: The night-flowering catchfly, an increasingly uncommon plant of arable fields, is one of the few wildflowers in Britain that opens its flowers at dusk

Above: The narrow road between Osmotherley and Hawnby cuts across the moor and then dips steeply to negotiate the narrow valley of Blow Gill. The hillsides are heavily wooded with broadleaved trees, glorious in autumn

The final line of hills is the Tabular Hills, stretching from north of Helmsley almost to the coast at Scarborough. They skirt the southern boundary of the Park, rising gently from the Vale of Pickering and levelling out as flat as a table (hence the name). Although only a few miles in width, the sudden and abrupt edge of the Tabular Hills is a major feature in the landscape. From the top of this steep escarpment edge there are many memorable viewpoints looking northwards over the vast expanse of central moorland.

There are no mountains. Roseberry Topping, a craggy outlier on the western boundary, is the only individual hill that presents a popular and challenging climb. It rises high enough to be observed for many miles around and is known affectionately as Yorkshire's Matterhorn. The highest point in the Park lies in the Cleveland Hills, at just 1,490ft (454m) among the lonely expanse of Urra Moor, where an Ordnance Survey triangulation pillar marks the spot.

Opposite: Cropton stands at a 'gateway' to Rosedale, above the steep escarpment of the Tabular Hills. The road north out of the village presents some stunning views over the moorland landscape

Cutting into the spread of heather moorlands are numerable green fingers, where the waters draining off the central watershed have carved out a network of valleys – the dales. The result is not a landscape composed of a single, vast tract of heather, but rather a collection of high moors separated by narrow, intervening dales. All the moors are individually named. The larger moors usually take the name of the nearest village or hamlet. Beyond this, there is an intriguing list of names both for the smaller moors and the different areas or divisions of the larger moors.

Freedom, wildness and isolation are the enduring images of a sombre moorland view, but down in the sheltered dales things take on a different hue. Encouraging signs of civilisation appear. A patchwork of green fields, bordered by stone walls, spreads along the dale bottoms and up the dale sides to the limit of land improvement. Above the farmland, a band of bracken edges the dale and finally gives way to heather on the moor tops. A scattering of farmhouses and small woodlands punctuate the daleside scene; a huddle of red-roofed houses indicates the nearest hamlet or village.

There are over 100 villages in the North York Moors and just about everyone has their particular favourite. Although the economic reliance of village life on agriculture has waned, the heritage of the past has not been overshadowed by tourism provision. The essential character of these villages is cherished both by residents and visitors alike. It is just one of the many responsibilities of the National Park Authority to ensure that this essential character remains intact. Each settlement is a product of history with its own identity and its own mix of village hall, green, church, chapel, historical ruins, houses, cottages and lanes. Each village has a story to tell.

Above: In spite of the signboards for the 'Sun Inn' on two nearby buildings, the pub in Bilsdale has always been known by its original house name of Spout House. The old Spout House is a remarkable sixteenth-century cruck-framed house and one of the oldest buildings in the National Park

It is easy to recognise the traditional building materials that belong to this part of Yorkshire. The materials used are stone, usually sandstone in the north and limestone in the south; and clay pantiles add the definitive, colourful, red roofs. Thatch is still seen occasionally and a few villages exhibit the use of brick and slate. The latter materials were first transported into the area by rail during the nineteenth century. Brick and slate are notable in the villages in Esk Dale, along the railway line from Middlesbrough to Whitby which was completed in 1835.

Thanks to the combination of stone and pantile, the farmsteads, village houses and buildings in the North York Moors have an unmistakable air of warmth, solidity and colour. The special qualities of the built environment are every bit as important

as the natural landscape; they are part of it and form an essential feature in the character of the North York Moors. Some villages like Hutton le Hole and Rosedale Abbey are tourist honeypots, attracting great numbers of visitors during weekends and summer holidays.

There are no large towns within the boundary of the North York Moors National Park. A number of market towns exist around the fringes, as do the major seaside resorts of Scarborough and Whitby. In the case of Helmsley, about half of this popular market town lies within the confines of the Park. The other settlements of notable size are Thornton le Dale in the south and the two coastal villages of Robin Hood's Bay and Staithes. A string of settlements in the valley of the Esk reach an appreciable size, as does the village of Osmotherley in the west.

The North York Moors is one of the least populated areas in England and Wales. It has a total population of just 25,560 spread over an area of 554 square miles (1,436sq km). In common with many upland areas the geography of the area has not been favourable to the growth of large settlements. Mining for alum, jet and ironstone is a thing of the past but the Boulby potash mine, in the north-eastern corner, provides considerable employment. It is however the rural nature of the area that confirms its position in today's tourism market. Tourism has overtaken farming as the economic mainstay of the Park.

An intriguing network of country roads provides access into the dales and across the moors. Thanks to the provision of the Moorsbus service, it is possible to see the panoramic delights of moor and dale from the comfort of public transport. One of the most popular routes across the high moorland leads from Hutton le Hole to Castleton. En route is Ralph Cross, the emblem of the National Park, which stands almost at the geographical centre of the area.

Above: The traditional fishing boat of this coastline is the coble (pronounced 'cobble'), a modern version of the Viking longboat. The sharp, steep bows can cut through the heavy breakers and the overlapping plank construction ('clinker-built') ensures maximum strength Opposite: 'Queen of Watering Places' was the accolade given to Scarborough by the Victorians. It is England's oldest holiday resort

Visitors can still 'let the train take the strain' along two routes in the North York Moors. Keeping close company with the River Esk on its way to the sea is the Esk Valley Line that runs from Middlesbrough to Whitby. One of the country's most popular steam railway routes runs through the heartland of the moors. From Pickering to Grosmont there is the opportunity to re-live the days of steam and enjoy the beautiful scenery of Newton Dale.

Over many centuries, a traditional and slowly evolving system of farming has created England's green and pleasant farmland. This scene has been shattered in many parts of England during recent decades, due to economic and political pressures. Upland dales, as in the North York Moors, have been cushioned from the onslaught of certain changes simply because the land is what we call marginal. It is not capable of producing high yields by any economically viable system. The daleside scenery has become a precious resource – valued as much for its scenic attraction as for its farming.

To a large extent the system of land use in the high moors has changed very little. In other instances, change has been dramatic. Heather moorlands have been ploughed out for green pastures or conifer plantations. Land in the North York Moors was first acquired by the Forestry Commission in 1920 and about 15 per cent of the National Park is planted with conifers. Originally, the forests were not planned to provide a role in tourism but they have become an important and attractive recreational resource. The provision of routes for motorists, walkers, mountain bikers and horse riders has been added to the basic objective to produce timber.

At some stage in exploring this part of Yorkshire, visitors reach that mystical line where land and sea meet. Along the coastal boundary of the National Park – which excludes Scarborough, Whitby and Sandsend – there are 26 miles (42km) of dramatic scenery. The cliffs are rarely less than 200ft (60m). Left largely to nature, this is a coastline which rejoices in unspoilt splendour. Rock Cliff, near Staithes, is the highest point on the east coast of England. Here, the altitude is 656ft (200m) above the sea.

There are few roads that lead down to the coast and there are only three villages with direct access to the sea – Staithes, Runswick and Robin Hood's Bay. Houses keep tight against the steep cliffs and tight against each other, as though they needed communal strength against the threat of gravity and the sea. Narrow lanes, alleyways and steps separate the close-packed, characterful houses and cottages.

Over the last forty years, a number of surveys and discoveries have highlighted the exceptional importance of the North York Moors National Park for its wildlife, geology and archaeology.

Of some 850 species of plants that exist in the Park, there are populations of about thirty plants that are rare in Britain. Two invertebrates

Etched on the hillside of the Cleveland Hills near Ingleby Greenhow is the trackbed of the Ingleby Incline. This was the northern end of the Rosedale Mineral Railway that carried some 10 million tons of ironstone en route to the iron and steel works of Teesside and County Durham

found in the Park are threatened on a global scale. The area is a critical stronghold for the pearl-bordered fritillary butterfly, and surveys indicate that the North York Moors is important for a number of species (including otter, merlin and golden plover) all of which are of national and European importance.

There are 58 Sites of Special Scientific Interest (SSSIs) in the Park and 25 of these are designated for their outstanding geological and geomorphological significance. In particular, two areas of cliff are of international importance because of their contribution to the understanding of evolution, rock formation and past environments.

Records reveal some 12,000 archaeological sites and features in the National Park. The area is exceptionally rich in Bronze Age remains and the spread of their burial mounds indicates that these early agriculturalists settled right across the moors. Over 700 sites and features have statutory protection as Scheduled Ancient Monuments.

We all place different and sometimes conflicting priorities on our National Parks, depending upon whether we live there or use them as a place of work or to visit for recreation. Even the wisdom of Solomon could not find a way to satisfy everyone. Nevertheless, the prime objectives must always be to conserve and enhance the natural beauty, wildlife, cultural heritage and public access of the areas. Carrying out these duties will ensure that future generations will be able to enjoy the North York Moors just as much as we do today.

Above: Relatively open landscapes provide big skies that sometimes provide their own drama. The 'Mother of Pearl' clouds are rarely seen
Opposite: The pier at Saltburn

1 The rocks beneath: geology and scenery

On any journey through the North York Moors National Park you will be aware of changes in the scenery. Passing from one end to the other you move through the flat landscapes of the Hambletons, the richly wooded havens of the southern fringes, the patchwork of green fields in the dales, the bleak wilderness of the heather moors and finally, the impressively bold coastal cliffs. All these scenes have something to tell you about the rocks that lie beneath your feet. The countryside is like an open-air textbook, simply waiting to be observed and understood.

In the very first moments of enjoying the view across any piece of countryside, your impressions are influenced by the shape of the land. The background drama of the hills and valleys can be instantly appreciated. It is then that your eyes turn to seek out the detailed elements of lakes, rivers, cliffs, quarries, roads, railways, farming activities, field patterns, trees, hedges, stone walls, buildings and other signs of human habitation.

Starting from Sutton Bank in the south-west corner, we shall take a journey across the Park observing the landscape and explain its creation. In our journey we will observe a landscape created by a variety of rocks. With just minor exceptions, all these rock beds are sedimentary (formed from the accumulation of underwater sediments) and all belong to a period in geological history known as the Jurassic – which took place about 190 million years ago.

The Jurassic is the period made famous through books, television and films as the age of the dinosaurs. Someone has yet to discover a dinosaur skeleton in the area, but we do know that they were here because fossil footprints of some of these creatures have been found. Considerable numbers of other fossilised species can be found and the area is well known for the remains of ammonites – sea creatures related to the modern octopus and squid. For students of geology the North York Moors is a good training ground, and is regarded as a classic area for the study of the Jurassic period.

The bare vertical cliffs which stand guard around Sutton Bank can be seen from a distance of at least 20 miles (32km) to the west. They send out a strong signal which indicates the western boundary of the National Park. Most prominent of these cliffs is Whitestone Cliff but it is, however, poetic licence to describe it as 'white'. In direct sunshine, the cliff presents a gleaming tower of pale, creamy orange. The variations in the colour of the exposed rocks here are due partly to impurities, partly to weathering and partly to the different types of rock. These are layers of limestones and calcareous gritstones (coarse sandstones). There are no really pure limestones in the North York Moors and the limestones always contain impurities, such as iron or silica, which affect the colour of the rocks.

In March 1755, the rock falls at Sutton Bank were so severe that local people thought there had been an earthquake. It was reported that the ground shook and trembled for two days. This photograph shows the bare cliffs of Roulston Scar, near Sutton Bank. There are suggestions that an early medieval castle was built on top of Hood Hill

In the valley of the River Derwent is the prominent landmark of Howden Hill. Like other 'outliers', a capping of hard rock has protected the underlying softer strata to produce a conical hill

Opposite: Visitors to Sutton Bank enjoy the panoramic view that stretches across the Vale of Mowbray to the Yorkshire Dales. Glistening in the sun, below the cliffs, are the waters of Lake Gormire, and a steep hillside path leads down to the edges of the lake

Closer at hand you can see the fissures and joints in the rockfaces which create large, roughly cube-shaped blocks. Some blocks look to be on the point of collapse and indeed these cliffs have a history of rock falls.

These rock falls are the result of a line of weakness which develops at the junction of the calcareous gritstones and the underlying shales. The gritstones are porous and rainwater is able to seep steadily downwards. However, the shale beds are impermeable and as a result, at the point of contact of these two differing layers of rock, the water builds up and is forced to the surface. The continual pressure of water at the junction causes a deterioration in the stability of the rocks and rock falls become inevitable.

A short distance away from Roulston Cliff at the edge of the airfield is a broad-based, conical hill known as Hood Hill. This type of landscape feature is called an outlier and Hood Hill is a good example of how varying degrees of hardness in different rocks can shape the landscape. A harder rock will obviously resist erosion to a greater extent and stand out 'head and shoulders' above any surrounding softer rocks which are weathered away. That is what has happened here; the capping of hard rock proved more resistant and gave some protection to the layers beneath. Other classic outliers that can be seen in the Park include the well-known Roseberry Topping, Freeborough Hill in the north, and Howden Hill, near Langdale End in the valley of the River Derwent.

Glistening in the sun below the escarpment at Sutton Bank is the only natural lake of any significance in the North York Moors. As with many notable natural features, Lake Gormire is associated with some weird and wonderful legends. This includes the popular superstition that it is bottomless. People are also curious as to why there is no visible outlet from the lake. The answer is that the water drains underground and emerges as a spring a few miles further south. The existence of the lake can be explained by looking back in geological time.

Towards the end of the last glaciation, the Vale of Mowbray was filled by a glacier. Meltwater draining from the moorland snowfield scoured a channel for itself between the escarpment edge of the moors and the glacier. A small basin in this channel became blocked to the north after landslips from Whitestone Cliff, and to the south by a relatively resistant outcrop of rocks. Today, springs at the base of the cliffs supply water to maintain the level of the lake.

Another curiosity of the North York Moors is that, like the chalk downs of the south of England, it has its own giant turf-cut landmark. This is the White Horse of Kilburn, created in 1857.

Its creators did not entirely appreciate the problems that their creation would impose on future generations. The rock beds of the Berkshire Downs are made of chalk and the Hambleton Hills of limestone – two entirely different types of rock. The Kilburn horse was therefore immediately at some disadvantage. Firstly, the colour of the limestone beds on the Kilburn hillside is a dull grey. This meant that the horse had to be treated with a coating of lime to make it stand out in the landscape. Secondly, the Kilburn hillside is convex and the bulging nature of the feature causes the surface of the horse to be particularly vulnerable to erosion. Ever since its creation, this legendary Yorkshire figure has needing 'grooming' at some considerable expense and effort.

Another feature which the North York Moors shares with the downs of the south of England is racehorse training. On the road leading from Sutton Bank towards Cold Kirby you will notice large areas of grassland on either side of the road. These are used for the training of racehorses. The thin soils that develop on the limestone beds support a short, somewhat springy turf – ideal for horse-racing and training gallops. During the seventeenth and eighteenth centuries there was a well-established racecourse here on the Hambleton Down. From the 1750s, racegoers changed their interest in favour of the York racecourse, and the last race meeting on the windy Hambletons was held in 1811. However, there are still racing stables in operation and the 400-year-old tradition of exercising horses on the gallops continues.

There are thirteen villages along the A170 between Helmsley and West Ayton, all of which are located at the junction of the foothills of the Tabular Hills and the Vale of Pickering. Their existence is due to the availability of water – an essential need of human settlement. Rainwater falling on the Tabular Hills refreshes the light soils and

THE BIRTH OF THE KILBURN HORSE

A local man, Thomas Taylor, had left the village to work in London, and on a journey through Berkshire, he was impressed by the turf-cut figures which he saw on the hillsides. It prompted him to send a letter to his friend and village schoolmaster, John Hodgson, suggesting that a horse might be cut on the hillside near Kilburn. Thirty-one men of Kilburn cleared the hillside that was marked out by Hodgson and his pupils – and the village of Kilburn had its horse.

The White Horse of Kilburn is one of Yorkshire's best-known landmarks. It was carved on the hillside above the village of Kilburn in 1857

Top: Limestone cottages at Helmsley
Above: Commondale. Brick is a
relatively uncommon building
material in the North York Moors
Opposite: In summertime, the low
level of water in Hodge Beck in
Kirkdale may be completely drained
by the 'swallow holes' along its
limestone bed

FLOWERS OF THE LIMESTONE

The chalk hills of the south are
famous for their wealth of
wildflowers, and throughout the
Tabular Hills, wildflower enthusiasts
will soon recognise those plants which
have a special relationship to the
calcareous soil which develops on the
underlying limestone. Orchids such as
the common spotted, bee, and
pyramidal are indicators of limestone
grasslands. Among a host of other
lime-loving plants to be found in the
relatively dry limestone pastures are
common rock-rose, cowslip, eyebright
and common violet.

then drains easily through the limestone beds. At the Vale of Pickering, the limestone beds meet a deep bed of impervious clays. Suddenly, the passage of the underground water is halted and an underground reserve of water builds up which eventually reaches the surface as springs. For this reason, the villages are often referred to as spring-line settlements.

Where the old route of the A170 crosses Kirkdale, near St Gregory's Minster, the ford over the limestone river bed is sometimes as dry as a bone and sometimes an impassable deep river. On a walk up Riccal Dale, near Helmsley, you will also see sections of a river bed where there is no water. This is typical of small streams and rivers which cut their course through a belt of limestone. Limestone is the only common hard rock which can be dissolved by the weak acids in rainwater. This acidity is sufficient to slowly dissolve the limestone along its joints and bedding planes. When a fissure becomes large enough to take a volume of water which matches the river flow, the river disappears down a 'swallow hole', and a network of underground channels and caves is created by the water draining through the limestone.

Alongside the ford at Kirkdale there is a wooded hollow which is floored with a jumble of large, overgrown rocks. These are the clues that indicate some nineteenth-century quarrying for limestone. High on the bare rock face is a letter-box-shaped opening that looks like the narrow entrance to a cave. Nothing too remarkable about that you might think. Yet this tranquil, unsung corner of Yorkshire revealed some shattering revelations during the early 1800s, for it proved to be the foundation of truths about climatic changes in geological history.

The cave was discovered in the limestone rockface by workmen quarrying in Kirkdale for roadstone in 1821. Scattered among the mud sediments of the cave floor was a massive collection of animal bones and teeth. Some of the bones were simply carted away with the stone and laid on the local road. But curiosity was driven a step further by a local doctor, John Harrison, and his friend John Gibson, a visitor from London, who saw the bones in the newly-made road. Word soon spread concerning the strange animal bones discovered in the cave. Samples were sent to Dr William Buckland, lecturer in geology at Oxford University, who travelled north to investigate the site for himself.

With great enthusiasm, Buckland and his assistant climbed into the cave equipped with flame torches and candles. They scrambled and crawled through a passage, discovering two or three larger chambers. Thousands of animal bones were preserved in the mud floor, along with hundreds of encrusted animal droppings. Buckland identified the bones of straight-tusked elephant, hippopotamus, narrow-nosed rhinoceros, tiger, bison, horse, deer, wolf, fox, rabbit or hare, weasel, rodents, some birds and the remains of nearly 300 hyenas. But how did any of the large animals squeeze their way through a 3ft (1m) wide cave entrance? The Oxford geologist declared that Kirkdale cave had simply been a den where hyenas had dragged the carcasses of the larger animals and devoured them.

Not only did Buckland's discoveries make him the most famous scientist in England at the time, but he also caused a huge sensation with his theory on why the den became disused. He claimed that the end came about with the world-encompassing flood exactly as told in the Book of Genesis. This refuelled the long-standing debate among scientists, clerics and the public on the literal truth of the Bible.

Within twenty years of Buckland's discovery however, the scientists agreed that England had at one time enjoyed a distinctly warm if not sub-tropical climate. Also, that the migration of the large, sub-tropical animals into Britain was completed before the formation of the North Sea marooned them forever. What had ended the hyenas' feastings was an enormous change in climate with the onset of the last glaciation. With the start of the big freeze, the den had been abandoned.

Leaving the A170 and taking the road north out of Kirkbymoorside to Gillamoor, you climb the dip slope of the Tabular Hills. This rising ground soon becomes as flat as a table – hence the name Tabular. Stretching from Helmsley to Oliver's Mount at Scarborough, the Tabular Hills stamp their character on the landscape even though they are only a few miles in width. Their most dramatic feature is the steep, north-facing escarpment which abruptly marks their northern limit. Their sphinx-like headlands seem to stand as silent sentries, guarding against entry from the expanse of heather moorland to the north. From the top of the escarpment edge there are superb panoramic views looking northwards over the central moorlands. At Gillamoor, the view is so sudden and unexpected that it provides the much-loved 'Surprise View'.

The strangely abrupt end to the Tabular Hills is a result of a long period of erosion during the geological history of the North York Moors. Originally, the limestone beds covered the whole of the area, but millions of years of erosion by rain, rivers, ice and wind gradually denuded the limestone and gritstone beds from the central and northern parts of the moors.

The central part of the North York Moors National Park is dominated by seemingly boundless tracts of heather-clad upland – for most visitors, the great glory of the moors. This obvious and dramatic change from the Tabular Hills reflects the change in the rock beds as clearly as any geological map. Limestone has given way to a series of sandstones with interbedded shales. It is these sandstone beds which are responsible for the essential character of the glorious heather moorlands. On the acid sandstones there are few plants that can match the special adaptation of heather to the harsh physical conditions of the moors. Heather dominates the scene for many miles and in late summer, a rich purple blanket clothes the entire landscape.

Some of the most dramatic features in the world's landscape are caused by the forces of moving ice and running water, and among the relatively rolling landscapes of the North York Moors, there are some notable features which owe their origin to these erosive powers. Newton Dale is the most dramatic valley in the moors, and is enjoyed by those who take the railway line from Pickering to Goathland and Grosmont. Today, only a tiny stream runs through this valley and it could never have

Above: In 1821, a limestone cave in Kirkdale revealed astonishing new evidence of prehistoric animals, but all that can be seen of the cave today is a letter-box-shaped opening
Right: The steep, north-facing escarpment edge of the Tabular Hills provides one of the most scenic features in the National Park.

produced sufficient power to create Newton Dale. In fact, this dale was created towards the end of the Ice Age, about 10,000 years ago. The erosive power of millions of gallons of meltwater from the moorland snowfield draining southwards in the direction of Pickering carved out this huge channel.

The heavily wooded valley known as Forge Valley, near Scarborough, has always been popular for its spring flowers and variety of woodland birds. The valley carries the River Derwent, a river that defies all logic in its choice of route to the North Sea. Near Hackness, just 5 miles (8km) from the coast, the Derwent shuns its original and most obvious route and undertakes 50 miles (80km) of whimsical wandering through Forge Valley, across the Vale of Pickering and over the Vale of York before it joins the Ouse, downstream of Selby. This is once again due to the situation which existed at the end of the Ice Age. The meltwaters from the moors found that the original and direct course of the River Derwent to the sea was blocked by a glacial ice sheet near the coast. A lake built up in the Hackness valley and eventually the meltwaters overflowed southwards to create Forge Valley and drain into the Vale of Pickering. Without doubt, Newton Dale and Forge Valley are two of the best examples of meltwater channels in the country.

Our journey across the Park now takes us eastwards to the coast. The relentless erosive power of the sea has bared the strata of the rocks along the high cliffs. It gradually erodes the less-resistant layers of sandstone and shale to make a ragged, rocky coastline. Every year, the high seas continue to crash against the cliffs and every year another part of the coast erodes. The shale beds along the coast are notoriously unstable. In December 1829 a major disaster occurred when parts of the cliff line collapsed to the south of Runswick Bay and the whole village of Kettleness slipped into the sea. In recent times, major sea defences have been necessary to protect the existing coastal settlements.

Only in a couple of places does the heather moorland reach the coastal cliffs. Instead we find a belt of good farmland running up to the North Sea cliffs. The land

Above: The impressive scale of the steep-sided valley of Newton Dale is emphasised in this aerial view. The valley was created, not by normal river erosion, but by millions of gallons of meltwater draining off the moorland snowfields towards the end of Ice Age
Right: Rich farmland occupies the Derwent valley bottom near Hackness, flanked on either side by the limestone uplands of the Tabular Hills. Although only 5 miles (8km) from the sea, the Derwent turns southwards here and flows through Forge Valley

DEEPEST MINE IN EUROPE

Potash and rock salt are mined from rocks at depths of between 3,600-3,900ft (1,100-1,200m) at the Boulby mine. It reputedly has the deepest mine shaft in Europe and is the only source of potash in the UK. Thousands of tons of potash are mined every day and mining extends to a distance of 2 miles (3km) under the North Sea.

Above: A treatment plant, tall chimneys, mine shafts and rail loading facility mark the location of the Boulby potash mine
Opposite above: A belt of good farmland – on boulder clay – runs along the coastal stretch of the National Park at Fylingthorpe
Opposite below: Extensive quarrying for alum resulted in the loss of half the headland at Kettleness Point. All that remains are the heaps of shale waste
Pages 32-3: At low tide, an impressive wave-cut platform is revealed extending into Robin Hood's Bay. An original dome-shaped landform, centred out in the bay, has been eroded away. The concentric circles of small ledges are known locally as 'scars'

here is covered by 'foreign' soils that owe their origin not to the underlying sandstone, but to a material called boulder clay which was brought here from elsewhere. This state of affairs is due to another aspect of the last glaciation. Encased within the coastal glacier was a mix of material eroded from the Lake District, Scotland and even Scandinavia. With the onset of warmer conditions, the glacier melted and the mix of clays, sands and gravel was simply dumped on the landscape.

North of Whitby along the coast road we reach the end of the bay at the appropriately named village of Sandsend. Along the cliffs are the unmistakable clues to the most extensive extractive industry in the history of the North York Moors. Huge, scrub-covered mounds can be seen near the prominent headland of Sandsend Ness. The beds of shale were quarried for the production of alum, a chemical used in the textile and leather industries. Alum was vital to the textile industry as a substance that fixed the coloured dyes to the cloth. From the early 1600s and for almost 300 years there were over twenty quarries on the moors which were worked for the production of alum. Millions of tons of shale were quarried. Alum production in England was exclusive to the North York Moors until a cheaper process was found in the 1870s using coal waste available at the collieries.

It is very easy to trace the scenery of the North York Moors and sense the natural beauty of the landscape. What may escape your notice is the importance which mining and quarrying has played in the history of the area. In times gone by, these moors have yielded alum, coal, ironstone, jet, limestone, sandstone and whinstone. Added to this impressive list are the reminders that moorland ironstone gave impetus to the iron and steel industry of Middlesbrough; the finest moorland stone was in demand for buildings in London, and 'Whitby' jet was world-famous in the heyday of Victorian jewellery. Village houses and drystone walls provide ample evidence of the local sources of limestone and sandstone, which have been used since earliest times.

In the north-east corner of the National Park near Staithes, a complex of buildings and chimneys indicate the location of another important industry. This is the Boulby potash mine, which is claimed to be one of the most sophisticated and efficient mines in the world. Potash from the North York Moors is supplied on a worldwide basis for agricultural fertilisers and for the chemical industry. Rock salt is also produced extensively for winter de-icing and maintenance of roads in the UK and abroad. The great mining tradition of the moors continues into the twenty-first century.

No account of the geology of the North York Moors would be complete without a tribute to the local man who achieved the status of 'The Father of English Geology'. He was William Smith who worked as a land agent for the Hackness estate and later retired to Scarborough where he died in 1839. Smith undertook meticulous observations of the rock beds, the fossils, the landscape, and the flora and fauna in the area. He was able to show how fossils could be used to identify individual rock beds to produce a relative timescale and make geological maps.

As described above, there is a great choice of countryside to explore in the North York Moors. It is one of the statutory duties of the National Park Authority to help everyone to enjoy and understand this beautiful area and help is on hand for the interested visitor. An invaluable starting point for many will be one of the National Park Centres which are found at Danby (The Moors Centre), Sutton Bank and Robin Hood's Bay (the Old Coastguard Station – run jointly with the National Trust). Visitors to the coast will find the new centre at Robin Hood's Bay – at the very edge of the sea – equally useful. The exhibitions and displays in these centres can give some useful background before you start your own explorations. Or you can go on a discovery walk to enjoy some first-hand interpretation with the help of a local expert.

2 Climate, vegetation and wildlife

Above: The rolling Cleveland Hills, seen here from above Battersby, provide an obvious western boundary to the North York Moors Opposite: The sense of wilderness lies in the heartland of the moors. Wide expanses of moorland stretch for miles to the horizon

The distinguished Yorkshire writers, Ella Pontefract and Marie Hartley, once wrote of a journey through the North York Moors when they experienced a summer haze that 'turns the valleys into blue mysterious country'. They seem to have ignored the harsher conditions which exist on the moors in winter, such as the pervading moorland 'roaks'. This is the local name for the wet fogs which cloak the high ground with a dank, eerie silence, completely robbing you of your sense of direction. Just as unpleasant are the icy blasts of the winter north-easterlies which sweep unhindered across the expanse of moorland, from the North Sea coast to the Tabular Hills.

Allowing for its position in the north-eastern corner of England, the North York Moors is fairly dry. It is also relatively mild in summer and cool in winter. In Britain, wind, rain and snow come mainly from the west. However, by the time the prevailing westerly winds reach the moors they have already shed a great deal of their moisture as rain or snow over the Pennines. In the rain-lashed fells of the Yorkshire Dales, annual rainfall will reach 60in (1,524mm). This compares with a maximum of around 45in (1,143mm) in the heart of the North York Moors. At lower altitudes around the edges of the Park, the rainfall is just 30in (762mm) annually.

Less rain generally means fewer clouds and the benefit of longer hours of sunshine. Like other areas of eastern England, the Park can generally expect relatively mild, dry summers. Nevertheless the North Sea has a marked influence on the area's climate. This is most telling when a change in the wind direction brings the north-easterlies blowing across the region. In summer, these breezes are cool and may bring sea fogs floating inland. In winter, the north-easterlies bring blasts of ice-cold air that cut clean across the high ground, making a blizzard seem ten times worse.

Variations in the weather always provide a topic of conversation. Differing weather reports are exchanged on places that are separated by only a few miles. The reason for these differences is often due to altitude. There are times, particularly from October to April, when a height difference of just 250ft (76m) can have a considerable effect on conditions. Folks in Kirkbymoorside can be blissfully unaware of a dank mist or a dusting of early snow that lies around Fadmoor and Gillamoor, situated only 250ft higher.

We are all aware that the higher you climb the colder it gets. Altitude varies in the North York Moors from sea-level to almost 1,500ft (457m) on the high moorland. Given that temperature decreases with an increase in altitude at a rate of about 1.6°C every 1,000ft (305m), we can expect to find differences between moorland and dale throughout the year. The theoretical reduction in temperature from the edges of the Park to the high moors amounts to some 1.6-2.2°C. Most importantly, this can be accentuated by higher wind speeds and greater cloud cover. The reality of this situation is very obvious to anyone who sets out on a country walk to higher ground. Extra clothing is advisable, if not essential.

As mentioned above, one of the most notable phenomena of the weather in the North York Moors is the roak. To say 'there's roak coming in' means that the moors will soon be shrouded in a damp mist. It comes in from the sea and moves inland, hugging the high ground across the moors. Its approach can be observed at the coast, particularly during summer. A dark line of mist is seen first out at sea, and it creeps towards the coast under the warm air of a summer's day.

Sun, water and wind are basic elements of climate. They are also basic to the distribution of all normal flowering plants. In addition, plants need nutrients. The natural supply of nutrients depends largely on the constituents of the bedrock, after it has weathered down into soil. All plants are at the mercy of

SWEARING LIKE BILLY-O

The severity of one moorland snowstorm resulted in a description of 'swearing' which has survived the passing of the last nine centuries, and is still sometimes heard today. In the autumn and winter of 1069, William the Conqueror and his army ravaged the countryside of the North Riding of Yorkshire and parts of County Durham. Such was the devastation that it became known as the 'Harrying of the North'. They were returning from Teesmouth to York, most probably along the western edge of the moors along the Hambleton Drove Road, when a severe snowstorm completely disorientated the company. In appalling conditions, William and six of his mounted escort were separated from the main contingent during the whole night. Such was the outburst of foul language from William that it gained a widespread reputation. It became common to describe a person given to bad language, in reference to the king, that he or she 'swears like 'Billy-O' or 'Billy Norman'.

THE DREADED ROAKS

The Yorkshire roaks are notorious – they were even dreaded by the Vikings who crossed the North Sea to raid and plunder the coast. In folk tales, roaks are the cause of souls lost, sometimes forever, in the moorland wilderness. A heavy roak is most unpleasant, with visibility down to a few yards, the air heavy and a chill dampness that penetrates quickly.

A SPECIAL AREA

In recognition of the internationally important numbers of breeding merlin and golden plover on the moors, the North York Moors as been designated a Special Protection Area (SPA). This is a European designation for areas specifically important for birds.

Above: Toothwort is a parasite, taking nourishment from a host plant, often a hazel tree. Its deathly pallor gives rise to the name of 'corpse flower'
Below left: There are three main species of heather on the moor: ling (the most common), cross-leaved heath and bell heather
Below right: Tormentil – a colourful sight along the close-cropped verges of the moorland roads

THE LIFE OF HEATHER

Heather is a dry, tough and wiry plant. Its success is largely due to its special physical and growth characteristics. To survive in the nutrient-starved soils, the heather makes minimal demands. Heather grows slowly, taking twenty-to-thirty years to reach old age and a height of 2-3ft (0.6-0.9m) when the stems become quite woody and 'leggy'.

these physical conditions, and in the North York Moors we can see that the distribution of vegetation reflects something of this link between geology and climate.

Ever since the North York Moors was designated a National Park in 1952, a major responsibility placed upon the Authority has been to ensure the conservation of the Park's predominant wildlife habitat – the heather moorland. This would be simply a pipe-dream without the interplay of two crucial factors – legislation and finance. Thanks to the pressure for legislation, the efforts and funding for moorland projects from the National Park Authority and the co-operation of the landowners, the central heartland of the moors has been recognised as being nationally important for wildlife. In December 1998, more than 170 square miles (44,000ha) of heather moorland was designated as a Site of Special Scientific Interest (SSSI).

Vital to its duty to protect the moorland is the need for the National Park Authority to obtain financial support from the European Union. The SSSI and SPA designations will undoubtedly help the Authority in obtaining funding to continue its conservation management projects.

On first impressions, the North York Moors' wide expanse of heather looks entirely natural. That is true to some extent, for it has been in this state for a very long time – about 2,500 years. However, these heather moors are not the creation of nature, they are the creation of man. And their story goes back to prehistoric times.

We know that the Bronze Age people lived and farmed on the high ground in considerable numbers. They slashed and burned the native woodland to create fields for growing crops and rearing animals. As soon as the fields were depleted in fertility, they moved on to create another clearing. A system of farming which uses up the soil nutrients but does not replace them will eventually fail, and after about 1,400 years disaster was inevitable. In addition, there was a marked deterioration in the climate to colder and wetter conditions towards the end of the Bronze Age. This hastened the abandonment of the high moors in favour of the valley slopes.

With its soil rendered infertile, the treeless high ground became fit for one particular plant which can survive in wet, cold and very acid conditions – and that plant is heather. Some other areas of the plateau were colonised by rough grassland and, in the wetter ground, by cotton grass.

These conditions persisted until the middle of the nineteenth century when steps were taken to increase the dominance of heather. With the popularity of grouse shooting from the 1850s onwards, landowners were keen to increase the

spread of heather which in turn would support greater numbers of grouse. This was achieved by burning areas of ground on a ten-to-twenty-year rotation to encourage the growth of new and nutritious shoots of heather. In addition, long runs of drainage ditches were dug over the wetter ground.

In the minds of most people, the North York Moors is inextricably associated with heather. During late August and early September the tiny purple flowers of the heather come into bloom and for a few weeks, the landscape becomes a purple carpet. According to one estimate there are as many as 3,000 million flowers to the square mile.

It is quite common to see small areas of heather in bloom during July. These early flowering heathers are either bell heather or cross-leaved heath, and can be distinguished fairly easily from common heather, or ling. All three have the typical bell-shaped flower but the bell heather, with its distinctly deep purple flowers, usually appears on drier ground on steeper slopes, boulders and bracken. Cross-leaved heath, on the other hand, with its larger, rose-pink flowers will be found in wetter areas. By far the most widespread heather is known as common heather, ling or Scottish heather. This is the heather which flowers in late August and has successfully colonised immense tracts of the high ground of the moors.

Fen Bog at the head of Newton Dale is an area of deep peat with notable bog and fenland plants. The bog presented great difficulty for the construction of the railway line. A combination of large timbers, heather and brushwood wrapped in sheep fleeces were sunk to create a causeway for the trackbed of the Whitby to Pickering railway

Above: Bog asphodel
*Below: Industrial activity came to
Esk Dale with the Middlesbrough to
Whitby railway in 1865. Brickworks
were established in Commondale
which lasted until the 1950s*

From a casual glance across the moors, you might think that heather was the only flowering plant present. Pure stands of heather can indeed be seen but in general there are other plants to be found. A notable favourite is bilberry – it has a characteristic purplish bloom on its black berry. The berry is gathered during July and August to make the delectable bilberry pies. Bilberry is another of the plants which adapts well to the acid soils of the moors, and it is often found growing as an understorey among the heather.

Ecologists describe the vegetation which grows on the high moors as belonging to two distinct plant communities – upland heath and upland bog. Both communities tolerate the acid soils of the moors. Among the heath communities in addition to the heathers are the so-called dwarf shrubs including bilberry, crowberry, cranberry, bog rosemary and bog myrtle. Distribution of these plants is determined by their adaptation to the drier and wetter areas of the moors. Rarities of these communities include dwarf cornel and bog rosemary.

When an area of ground is waterlogged for a greater part of the year, the normal decaying processes of dead vegetation slow down. The accumulation of slowly decaying organic material forms a layer of material known as peat. Acting like a sponge, the peat itself holds great amounts of rainwater and simply ensures the formation of even more peat. Some interesting plants of the peat bogs include insect-eating sundew and butterwort, marsh violet, bog asphodel, lesser

twayblade, bog myrtle and bog pimpernel. There are patches of rushes and cotton grass, but nothing to compare with the pure cotton-grass moors of the Pennines.

In spring there is an upsurge in the bird population of the moors. Lapwing, curlew, golden plover, redshank, snipe, wheatear and ring ouzel all return to their temporary moorland habitat to nest and breed. Large numbers of lapwing breed on the moors but they are not restricted to the high ground. They are aggressively protective of their nesting sites against any intruders, including humans.

Insect life is always associated with the vegetation. For example, it is not uncommon to see green and black caterpillars feeding on the heather during the early and middle summer. These caterpillars will pupate and emerge from their cocoons as richly coloured emperor moths. Typical butterflies of the moorland include the green hairstreak and the common heath.

There is just one poisonous snake native to Britain – the adder. Living on moors and heaths, the adder is a protected species, and it is a timid, wary creature, seen only on rare occasions. Also known as the viper, this snake will bite if any attempt is made to take hold of it. Anyone bitten by an adder needs to be taken immediately to the nearest doctor or hospital, but the best plan is to leave these harmless creatures well alone.

THE RED GROUSE
Of all the wildlife associated with the heather moorland, the most synonymous is the red grouse. It used to be called quite simply the 'moor bird'. This is claimed to be the only bird that is unique to Britain (but it has been introduced into Belgium). No other bird is so characteristic of and dependent upon heather. The green shoots of young heather provide the bird with its staple diet. Old heather provides suitable nesting sites where the plumage of the grouse (dark reddish brown, spotted and barred with black) is effective camouflage. At close range, the males are seen to have a bold red comb over the eye and 'pyjama' legs, which are covered in white feathers.

When disturbed, the grouse bursts noisily into flight with rapid wing beats and then flies over the moor in a series of low glides and whirring flight at speed. Seldom long in flight, it returns to ground with its clear call of 'ge'bak, ge'bak, ge'bak, bak, bak, bak'. There is no mistaking its warning to 'get back!'

Pages 40-1: Broadleaved woodland
Above (left to right): Bird's nest orchid; Pyramidal orchid; Greater butterfly orchid
Below left: Wild daffodils
Below right: Bird's-eye primrose

FARNDALE DAFFODILS

There is one wildflower which captures the interest of thousands of visitors to the North York Moors. They arrive each spring to saunter from Low Mill to Church Houses in Farndale, where Nature celebrates a new season with a spectacular display of wild daffodils. A carpet of gold spreads along 7 miles (11km) of the dale. We tend to forget that the daffodil is a truly wildflower and it grows in many of the moorland dales and throughout Britain. It is always difficult to predict when the wild daffodils in Farndale will be at their best but you should check with the Tourist Information Centres. If you haven't been on a bus lately, then also check on the Moorsbus services which run into Farndale during the daffodil season. It is a good idea to go 'green' and travel without the problem of parking your car.

As we leave the high moors and come down to lower ground, the first plant which usually dominates the upper slopes of the dales is bracken. Bracken generally grows in a band that lies above the uppermost line of farm improvement and below the edge of the heather moorland. Bracken is a fern, one of the flowerless plants that reproduce by spores, not seeds. It spreads mainly by the growth of its creeping, underground rhizomes. Bracken is widely recognised as a vigorously invasive plant, potentially poisonous to animals and a financial wasteland to hill farmers. Bracken also produces spores that may have cancer-inducing properties, and the plant provides a habitat for a life-threatening sheep tick. Some people regard it as Britain's worst weed.

Is there anything good that can be said about bracken? Yes – and more than might be initially thought. Firstly it is a native plant that belongs to the drier parts of our uplands. With the overall loss of rough pastures in Britain, bracken has a conservation value as a habitat for small birds such as the whinchat. It also offers shelter for invertebrates such as butterflies, including some threatened species. Few people would argue with the fact that bracken adds considerable scenic interest to the landscape of the Park. During autumn, the dales are edged with a strip of rich russet, turning to burnished copper as the bracken dies down in the frosts. In spring the young green fronds uncurl to provide a line of fresh lime-green to signal the awakening of a new season.

By far the richest area for plant life lies along the southern edge of the National Park. This is essentially limestone country, stretching from Sutton Bank in the west to the Hackness Hills, near Scarborough, in the east. Some of our most attractive wildflowers grow in this 30-mile (48km) long belt of ground which is about 2-3 miles (3-5km) in width. The dry grassland and disused quarries provide habitats for a wealth of plants including rock rose, salad burnet and bloody cranesbill, as well the fascinating bee and fly orchids. In the wet limestone meadows are such delights as the bird's-eye primrose, butterwort, globe flower, marsh helleborine and marsh orchid.

There is a clear distinction between the two broad categories of woodland – coniferous woodland and broadleaved woodland. Together they cover more than a fifth of the National Park. Approximately 15 per cent of the National Park is planted with coniferous woodland for commercial forestry. Although broadleaved woodland only covers 7 per cent of the Park, it holds a far greater diversity of wildlife. A Woodland Advisory Service provided by the Park Authority aims to encourage good management of the existing broadleaved woods and funds projects to develop new native woodlands.

Since prehistoric times, there has been a continuing reduction in Britain's woodland cover. It was not until the 1920s that this situation was reversed in the North York Moors. Given a remit to produce timber on a commercial basis, the

Above (left to right): Fly orchid; Bee orchid; Marsh helleborine
Below: Female emperor moth
Below left: Slow worm
Below right: Lapwing

Walking vertically down a tree trunk is as easy to the nuthatch as climbing up it

BIRDS OF THE COAST

As might be expected, it is the seabirds that provide the prime widlife interest along the towering coastal cliffs. Easily observed are the herring gull, kittiwake (pictured below) and fulmar. Life for the fulmar looks fairly effortless as it glides majestically along the air currents close to the cliff face. Recorded summer sightings along the coastline also include bar-tailed godwit, cormorant, common sandpiper, common tern, dunlin, oystercatcher, redshank, rock pipit and turnstone.

Forestry Commission purchased land for the planting of coniferous woodland, and a new habitat was created.

In the middle period of a forest's life, the interior of a pure coniferous woodland is a dark place. With little light there is little wildlife. However, along the forest rides and among plantations that are young, old, mixed or cleared, there are habitats for many species of wildlife. Roe deer have found a home in the forest but sightings of this shy and suspicious animal are relatively rare. Birds such as crossbills, coal tits, long-tailed tits, jays, siskins and sparrowhawks all find suitable nesting sites. One rare bird which has come to nest in the scrub layer of cleared or recently planted conifer forests is the nightjar. While flying only at twilight and through the night, it feeds on the forest's high population of moths. This summer visitor from central Africa can be identified by its strange rhythmical 'churring' trill – if you are out there in the dark of night!

Ancient broadleaved woodland is generally confined to sections of river valleys where the sides are too steep for cultivation. In a few cases, they are the remnants of woodland deliberately preserved in earlier times as hunting ground and sources of timber for fuel, furniture, houses, ships and tools. We can find these woodlands today in the eight sister dales which cut their narrow, steep-sided valleys through the Tabular Hills. In addition, some of the sections of the River Esk and its tributary valleys provide picturesque woodland – for example Arncliff Woods near Glaisdale, Ellerbeck and West Beck near Goathland. Beautiful and rare species of wildflowers are found in the herb layer of the broadleaved woodlands of the limestone belt. Baneberry, bird's-nest orchid, columbine, herb Paris and yellow star of Bethlehem mix with a host of more common woodland plants.

The rivers of the North York Moors support a rich variety of habitats and wildlife. Some of the animals and birds that make a home in these habitats are specially protected because they are rare or threatened in Britain. Otter, water vole, kingfisher and dipper are all found in the Park. The River Esk is particularly important as the only river in Yorkshire that is used by salmon and sea trout as a spawning ground. A deterioration in the quality of fishing and the loss of riverbank habitat due to erosion were recognised as problems along the Esk. Thankfully, the National Park Authority was able to obtain funding for a River Esk Regeneration Programme, and work continues to protect and enhance the river habitats. Thousands of salmon fry have been released into the river to improve the quality of the fishing. A similar project in the upper reaches of the River Derwent will assist in the conservation and management of that river.

There are no areas of sand dunes or salt marshes along the coastline of the North York Moors, neither are there are many true maritime flowers to be found. Nevertheless, the covering of boulder clay provides a habitat for a variety of common flowers, and small, steep-sided valleys punctuate the coastal region, providing pockets of herb-rich, broadleaved woodland.

Right: The headwaters of the River Rye run off the southern flanks of Snilesworth Moor in the Cleveland Hills. For much of its course, the river is hidden from roadside view

3 Man's influence

Below: Frank Elgee, a much-respected naturalist and archaeologist, left a record of his deep love and knowledge of the moors in his books. The Elgee Memorial Stone on Blakey Ridge was unveiled in 1953

Opposite: Man-made additions to the moorland landscape include numerous stone crosses and standing stones in a variety of shapes and forms. One such is the estate boundary stone known as the Margery (or Margery Bradley) Stone on Blakey Ridge

The vast treeless plateau at the heart of the North York Moors offers no obvious incentive for human settlement, and the miles of moorland seem to present a relatively inhospitable environment. This is the land of the red grouse and the moor sheep which alone can face the ice-cold blasts of winter and survive until spring. Yet this vast area of heather has sustained large communities of people, and it is a story that takes us back many thousands of years to the Stone Age.

Evidence of the story of human settlement in the North York Moors can still be found in the landscape of today. There are records of some 12,000 archaeological sites and features in the area, of which over 700 are given statutory protection as Scheduled Ancient Monuments. Through its policies, plans, consultations, management agreements and assistance, the National Park Authority undertakes to ensure that the archaeological and historical resources of the Park are protected and conserved. This is an area that is exceptionally rich in archaeological and historical interest and these resources provide us with clues to our understanding of the past.

About 10,000 years ago, the last vestiges of Arctic weather retreated from Britain. The Great Ice Age had ended and life was set to reappear on the land-

scape. With temperatures rising above 5.5°C, plant life was gradually re-established and animal and human life also returned. Britain at this time was part of the great European land mass.

From about 8000BC communities of Middle Stone Age people started an overland migration into the area of present-day England. However the continued melting of the ice cap and the consequent rise in sea-level finally resulted in a separation. The North Sea was complete by about 5000BC and from that time onwards, waves of settlers from mainland Europe had to arrive in England by boat.

The story of human settlement in the moors is very much related to the picture of vegetation history. Evidence of that vegetation history lies hidden within the thousands of pollen grains preserved in the moorland peat. Using radiocarbon dating of the pollen grains, we can describe with some confidence the actual species of plants and trees that existed at various times through the millennia.

There is not much evidence of the first people who arrived on the moors. A widespread scattering of flint tools and barbed flint flakes used in spears and arrows are the only relics of their culture. Their hunting and gathering way of life was fairly basic. Food was obtained by hunting, fishing and gathering plant foods. Discoveries of the flints over a wide area indicate that they hunted throughout the moors. These people belonged to the Mesolithic (Middle Stone Age) period, dated from about 8000 to 4500BC.

END OF THE WILDWOOD
From the radiocarbon dating of pollern grains, we know that by 4000BC the North York Moors was almost completely covered with a mixed oak forest. The question is – what caused its disappearance? The short answer is that the forest cover was destroyed by the arrival of communities intent on creating farmland.

The first significant step in destroying the forest cover was made during the Neolithic (New Stone Age) period that began around 4500BC and ended around 2000BC. New settlers continued to arrive from the east throughout this period. With an increase in population and the introduction of agriculture, areas of the forest began to be cleared on a permanent basis. These first farmers grew crops, kept farm animals, made pottery and became highly skilled in making stone implements. Their settlements were concentrated in the best farmland, particularly on the Tabular Hills. These areas have been continuously farmed ever since. Not surprisingly, the activities of farming over the centuries has obliterated much of the evidence of our Neolithic ancestors. There are only about a dozen of their distinctive 'long barrows' still surviving. These were their burial mounds, and are composed of long, low mounds of earth and stones.

As with any phase in human history, there is no overall, sharp break between the various prehistoric cultures. Around 2000BC a group of people known as the Beaker People (named from their distinctive pottery beakers) arrived in Britain. They began the change from the Neolithic to the Bronze Age (around 2000 to 600BC). The final destruction of the original forest in the North York Moors was made during this 1,400-year period of the Bronze Age. Over this time the new influx of people from the European continent made their fields and their homes right across the moors. They systematically destroyed the woodland by slashing and burning their way through the original wildwood. An important clue to the spread of settlement at this time is that there was a warmer and drier climate at the start of the Bronze Age. For the first time, it was possible to live on the high plateau throughout the year.

But there was never any attempt to replace the nutrients in the soil. Having exhausted one patch of land, the Bronze Age farmers simply moved on to grow their crops and graze their animals in the next clearing. Eventually there was no fertile land left. Another reason for abandoning the high ground was that the climate took a step back – it became much colder and wetter. Robbed forever of their natural fertility, the high plateaux were left to be colonised by a heathland vegetation.

Since the end of the Bronze Age in around 600BC, there has been no widespread human disturbance across much of the upland heath in the North York Moors. As a result, some notable evidence survives of the Bronze Age people. In particular, there are about 3,000 Bronze Age burial mounds or barrows. About 200 of them have been excavated and records made of their grave goods. Digging out the burials was a favourite Victorian pastime and unfortunately many were 'robbed' of their contents without any record of the finds.

Another sign of the Bronze Age people on the moors are the many cairnfields and dykes. The cairnfields are collections of stone heaps which appear in random formation, and were probably just irregular field clearances. Dykes are prehistoric ditch-and-bank earthworks. Some are quite complex, fairly well preserved and can extend up to 6 miles (10km) in length. The precise purpose of the dykes remains a mystery but they seem to indicate some territorial division of land.

The Iron Age dates from approximately from 600BC to AD50 and takes its name as the period during which iron replaced bronze in the making of implements and weapons. During this period, there was a spread of occupation in the valleys and across the Tabular Hills. Evidence of this occupation is relatively sparse but that is not entirely surprising. Over the last 2,000 years these areas have been resettled, ploughed and exploited many times over. Iron Age settlers

THE HOWES OF THE MOORS

Variously referred to as round barrows, howes and tumuli, the Bronze Age burials may vary from slight bumps in the heather to large circular shaped mounds, up to 8ft (2.5m) high and 65ft (20m) in diameter. In the North York Moors the larger burials have become known as howes, from the Scandinavian haugr for burial mound. Some of them can be found on the Ordnance Survey maps of the area and have individual names such as Kettle Howe, Loose Howe, Lilla Howe and Pike Howe.

Opposite: Prehistoric ditch on the moor above Newton Dale: there are few clues as to the precise purpose of the ditch-and-bank earthworks that are found in the moors

WADE'S CAUSEWAY

On Wheeldale Moor, the foundations of part of the road known as Wade's Causeway have survived. It has long been quoted as one of the best preserved and longest stretches of Roman road in Britain. However, recent research has cast some uncertainty about the date of its construction.

Above: Near Saltergate is a prehistoric double dyke on Whinny Nab

are noted for their hillforts elsewhere in Britain but we have records of only two promontory forts (now partly destroyed) at Boltby Scar and Roulston Scar that were probably Iron Age. There are, however, two 'chariot burials' which contained fragments of Iron Age chariots. There is also a collection of circular house foundations or stone 'hut circles' on Percy Rigg. Iron Age pastoral enclosures have been found on Great Ayton Moor and at Crown End, Westerdale. Iron 'bloomery' sites have been found on Levisham Moor and near Roxby.

Written history in Britain begins with the Romans, and the earliest invasions of 55BC and 54BC by Julius Caesar. The history of Britain is a series of successful conquests and settlement by invaders from Europe. Following the first-century conquest by the Roman army, a long list of invaders sailed across the North Sea. There were Angles, Saxons, Danes, Vikings and finally Normans who made the last successful invasion of England in AD1066. All these people left their mark among the Yorkshire moors and dales.

In AD43, the armies of Emperor Claudius landed in south-east England, and the province of Britannia was added to the great Roman Empire. By AD71 the army had reached Yorkshire and set about building a legionary fortress at *Eboracum* (York). From their fort at *Derventio* (Malton), the Roman legionaries were poised to extend their influence into the North York Moors. This was all part of their strategy to conquer and control the various northern tribes, known collectively as the Brigantes.

A notable road-building programme is one of the clues to the success of the Roman occupation. These roads provided for the reasonably rapid movement of troops who could enforce the Roman rule. Radiating from Malton were a number of roads. One of these, known as Wade's Causeway, led north-eastwards over the Vale of Pickering and across the moors to the North Sea coast.

Associated with Wade's Causeway are the Roman camps at Cawthorn, north of Pickering and Lease Rigg, near Grosmont. A winter posting to the moors must have made many a Roman soldier wish for the warmth of his homeland in Italy. Dating from around AD100, the Cawthorn Roman camps are of particular archaeological interest and a trail leaflet is published by the National Park Authority. The site was purchased by the Authority in 1983 to protect and interpret one of the best examples of a complex of Roman training camps in the country. Recent investigations have revealed evidence of a later settlement on the site.

Along the Yorkshire coast the Romans built fortified look-out posts (signal stations) at Filey, Scarborough, Ravenscar, Goldsborough and Hunt Cliff. Built close to the coastal cliffs, these stations were on the look-out for a new army of invaders from across the North Sea. During the late fourth and early fifth centuries a number of tribes of Germanic people (in particular the Angles, Saxons and Jutes) made raids on the Yorkshire coast. At some time early in the fifth century, a group of sea-raiders defeated the Roman guards and destroyed the coastal signal stations. Very soon afterwards, the Roman occupation of Britain came to an end. The Roman empire was in decline and all the legionary forces in Britain were recalled to Rome by about AD410. At Scarborough, two-thirds of the foundations of the signal station are excellently displayed at the cliff edge in the grounds of Scarborough Castle.

With the end of Roman military and civilian services, the way was open for the Germanic tribes to arrive and settle without much opposition. Boat-loads of Angles, Saxons and Jutes arrived in family and tribal groups to seek the best farmland and build their homes. For the local population it was a case of either stay put and tolerate the new overlords, or leave home and migrate westwards.

Mass immigration of Angles, Saxons and Jutes, particularly during the sixth century, caused some notable changes. A new culture had arrived. The Celtic language and the terms Britons and Britain were replaced. The incomers called their new homeland *Englalond* – the 'land of the Angles' – and they introduced their Germanic language *Englisc*, which we refer to as Anglo-Saxon or Old English. The clearest evidence we have of our Anglian ancestors lies in the place names of the villages on the moors. Look, for example, at the number of settlements that have the ending 'ton'. This place name element is the modernised form of 'tun', an Anglian name for a homestead or farmstead. Along the Tabular Hills there are Carlton, Appleton-le-Moors, Sinnington, Wrelton, Middleton, Thornton le Dale, Wilton, Allerston, Ebberston, Snainton, Brompton and Ayton.

Although Christianity became a permitted religion throughout the Roman

Below: The Roman soldiers would have found a cold and windy camp site here at Cawthorn, north of Pickering. Their camps were built around AD100

Above: At the edge of the cliff headland, within the grounds of Scarborough castle, are the remains of a Roman signal station. The view remains spectacular

empire in AD313, there are no surviving remains of churches or related items from this period in the National Park. When the pagan Anglo-Saxons arrived in the fifth century, Christianity suffered a setback for the next 200 years. The new society worshipped a number of gods, particularly Woden, the god of war. However, Christianity returned to Yorkshire in the seventh century when King Edwin of Northumbria was baptised in York on Easter Day, AD627.

The prime symbol of the Christian religion has always been the cross, and the North York Moors has the largest concentration of stone moorland crosses anywhere in Britain. Probably the oldest cross still standing on the moors is Lilla Cross, which dates back more than 1,300 years to the seventh century. Lilla, chief minister to King Edwin, was killed while saving the king from an assassin's

dagger in 626, the year before Edwin was baptised. In grateful recognition, Lilla was given a notable burial on Fylingdales Moor, and some time later, a stone cross was added in memory of his selfless act. Lilla Cross is claimed to be the oldest Christian monument in the north of England.

It is no exaggeration to say that the North York Moors was the cradle of Christianity in Yorkshire. Monasteries were established in the seventh century at Lastingham (654) and at Whitby (657). In addition a nunnery was built at Hackness in 680. Although we can see nothing of these Anglo-Saxon buildings today, the sites are of great interest because of rebuildings and buildings of a later date. Only a few relics remain in the moors, at Hackness and Kirkdale, that can take us back over thirteen centuries.

Peace seldom lasts for long. Life in the early monastic churches came to an end with the arrival of the Danes in the ninth century. Terminology can get confusing, but Danes and Norwegians are often referred to as Vikings or Scandinavians (and sometimes, Norsemen). During one of their raids in 867, the Danes

Above: Scottish cattlemen drove their herds to the English market towns. Part of their route between Scarth Nick and Sutton Bank is known as the Hambleton Drove Road
Opposite: On the moor above Rosedale Head is an estate boundary stone named White Cross. It is affectionately known as 'Fat Betty' because of the considerable girth of the base stone, and is associated in folk tales with nearby Ralph Cross

destroyed the religious centres at Whitby, Hackness and Lastingham. In the same year, the Danes defeated the Anglo-Saxons in battle at York and set up their new Danish kingdom based at *Jorvik* (York).

Despite their apparent initial ferocity, the Vikings soon settled down. Farmers, tradesmen and craftsmen migrated from Scandinavia and eventually they converted to Christianity and built churches. In a number of our present-day churches there are tombstones and cross fragments that reveal a Viking influence in their design and carvings. (These are sometimes referred to as Anglo-Saxon simply because they fall into the period before the Norman Conquest of 1066.)

Unmistakable, however, is that the Vikings introduced their language and named or renamed a number of settlements. In the Yorkshire dialect, hundreds of Viking words have survived and the place-name elements of the Viking period can be traced, for example in the endings of 'by' (from the Scandinavian word *byr*). Such villages as Boulby, Danby, Thimbleby, Boltby, Swainby, Thirkleby, Ingleby and Easby all indicate their Viking origin.

Before we leave the Anglo-Saxon period, we must return to one of the area's most interesting churches – Kirkdale Minster. Above the doorway

Above: North of Osmotherley are the remains of a monastic church and cells belonging to Mount Grace Priory. These are the best-preserved ruins of a Carthusian monastery in England
Right: The hamlet of Ellerburn is located in a delightful green valley near Thornton le Dale. The church has a number of carved fragments dating back to the Anglo-Danish period
Opposite: In a secluded, wooded setting is the eleventh-century church of St Gregory's Minster (or Kirkdale Minster). Above the doorway is the most complete example of an Anglo-Saxon sundial, inscribed in Old English

is probably the world's most important eleventh-century sundial. With a little determination you should be able to decipher a few words of the Old English inscription on the long slab of stone. It records the names of the king, the earl, the owner, the builder and the priest. From this information we can deduce that the church was built sometime between 1055 and 1065.

The 400 to 500-year period known as the Middle Ages is generally accepted as covering the eleventh to the fifteenth centuries. With a little extension we can provide two memorable dates relating to this period of English history. We shall begin with 1066 (the Norman Conquest) and end with 1536 (the Dissolution of the Monasteries).

On 14 October 1066, Duke William of Normandy fulfilled his claim to the English throne by defeating King Harold at the Battle of Hastings. From that day, the life of every person in England was to change. Within twenty years a Norman king and a few thousand Norman overlords had taken control of a nation of over a million people.

We can see their influence today in the North York Moors in the castles, monastic buildings and churches which belong to the Norman period. Central to the imposition of

the Norman rule was the building of castles. The best-preserved ruins of their castles can be seen at Helmsley, Pickering and Scarborough. Other castle ruins include Ayton Castle (near West Ayton), Danby Castle, Mulgrave Castle (near Lythe) and Whorlton Castle (near Swainby).

Once they had established their landownership, the Norman barons invited groups of monks to come over from France and gifts of land and money were made to them. What no one could foresee was that their enterprise would in time transform the monastic orders into notable landowners. Eventually, it was their success which contributed to their downfall. Henry VIII was envious of their wealth and by his Act of Dissolution in 1536, he began the dissolution of the monasteries. By 1540 all the English monasteries were closed. Something of the former wealth and glory of English monasticism can be seen today in the area of the North York Moors at Rievaulx Abbey, Byland Abbey, Whitby Abbey and Mount Grace Priory.

The search for wealth has been central to the story of human settlement throughout the ages. That search took a leap forward during the nineteenth century. The coming of the railways played a crucial part. Railways were built from Whitby to Pickering (opened 1836, closed 1965, then reopened between Pickering to Grosmont in 1973); Middlesbrough to Whitby (opened 1868), and Scarborough to Whitby (opened 1884, closed 1965).

Alongside the building of railways came the discovery of ironstone, the popularity of jet and the quarrying of limestone, whinstone and sandstone. Nature has masked many of the scars of nineteenth-century mineral exploitation of the

THE MEMORIALS OF HACKNESS AND KIRKDALE

Inside Hackness church there are two rare pieces of an Anglo-Saxon memorial cross that are both carved with long inscriptions. Abbess Oedilburga, an abbess at the seventh-century nunnery, is named in one of the inscriptions. There are two notable coffin lids or tomb-chest tops inside the little Kirkdale Minster near Kirkbymoorside. They present quite a puzzle. The beautiful and delicately inscribed patterns indicate the burial of some prominent person and you would expect to find them in an important ecclesiastical centre. It remains a mystery why they are here when there is no record of an early Anglo-Saxon religious house at this location.

Opposite: The extensive ruins of Rievaulx Abbey give some indication of the wealth of the Cistercian order in early medieval times. This unusual view of the abbey is taken from the north
Left: Helmsley Castle was built with an impressive array of defences – two deep ditches separated by a massive earthmound, a high surrounding stone wall, nine towers and a keep

Top: The massive stone archways of the Rosedale kilns are a relic of the ironstone mining bonanza of the nineteenth century
Above: An unsuccessful exploration for ironstone was made on the Farndale side of Blakey Ridge
Opposite: Radomes on Fylingdales Moor – replaced in 1992

moors. Such relics as the Rosedale kilns have become items of interest to the industrial archaeologist.

During the nineteenth century, landowners also took a renewed financial interest in the great expanse of moorland. From the 1850s, grouse shooting became a popular sport and gamekeepers were employed by the large estates. They began a system of periodic burning of patches of the moor to promote the stands of pure heather.

Despite its relatively isolated position, the North York Moors is not without people who have made their mark in English history. They may not have instant recognition but their names live on in the titles of the Father of English Poetry and of the English Sacred Song, the Father of the Modern Novel and the Father of Aeronautics. The moors have also raised one of the world's greatest sea captains and an oak woodcarver whose memory and craftsmanship lives on through his world-renowned trademark.

If you climb the famous 199 steps to reach Whitby Abbey, you will see a 20ft (6m) high cross as you gather your breath at the top. This richly carved, sandstone cross is a memorial to a seventh-century monk called Caedmon. His *Song of Creation*, created in a dream, marks him as the first identifiable author of English verse. For this reason he has become known as the Father of English Poetry and Father of the English Sacred Song.

And where did the world's story of aviation begin? Answer – on the doorstep of the North York Moors. Nearly 150 years ago, the dream of manned flight became a reality in the village of Brompton. Sir George Caley was the man responsible. In 1853 this brilliant inventor put his young coachman into an engine-less aircraft and made the first flight of man in a heavier-than-air machine. His theories of flight provided the basis for the development of the aeroplane and have earned him the title of the Father of Aviation.

Long before he tasted the salt sea air, the young James Cook was brought up on a farm overshadowed by Roseberry Topping, near the town of Great Ayton. He took to life at sea from the town of Whitby in 1746. Captain James Cook became a legend in his own lifetime and one of the most successful explorers the world has ever known.

Finally, is there a better wood in the world than good old English oak? To answer that we can turn to a twentieth-century craftsman in the little village of Kilburn. He has left a resounding testimony to the beauty of carved English oak through his furniture. Robert Thompson became known as 'The Mouseman' from the distinctive trademark he carved on all his work, and the workshops in Kilburn still continue his fine tradition of oak-carved furniture.

FATHER OF THE NOVEL

A visit to the village of Coxwold offers the chance to see Shandy Hall, once the home of an eccentric vicar and novelist called Laurence Sterne. His first two volumes of Tristram Shandy published in 1759 took the eighteenth-century literary world by storm. His international reputation is such that he is often acclaimed as the Father of the Modern English Novel.

4 Land use, culture and customs

Above: Changes in farming economics have seen the demise of many moorland farms. The intake land (reclaimed from the moor) will revert to moorland if it is left unattended

Every period of human history has been faced with changes to its land use, culture and customs, but during the twentieth century there was an unprecedented acceleration in the pace of change. In the North York Moors, the very nature of the moorland landscape and the area's limited natural resources tended to put a brake on the situation, and in common with many rural areas of England, a few traditions have stubbornly survived from earlier centuries.

For thousands of years, the economic mainstay of the North York Moors has been farming. Generations of farmers have made and maintained a farmed landscape that is a pleasure to see. The rural scene is a vital part of the attraction that draws over 11 million car-borne visitors every year to the North York Moors National Park.

But at the beginning of the twenty-first century, a cloud of uncertainty hangs in the minds of daleside farmers and there is serious concern over the financial state of our upland farms. In recent years the farming industry has suffered economic setbacks and the viability of hill farming in particular has declined. Since 1990, when the National Park Authority launched its North York Moors Farm Scheme, a system of grants has provided incentives for environmental conservation to be included as an integral part of a farming enterprise. This is a scheme which continues to assist in giving some improvement to farm incomes while providing a positive benefit to the landscape, wildlife and recreational use of the Park.

Next to tourism, farming is the second most important source of employment in the moors. In 1996, the Agricultural Census recorded a total workforce of 2,939 employed on 1,342 working farms. The greatest number of working farms (613) is found in the heartland of the area, where the dales cut deep into the central moorland. Grazing on the patchwork quilt of green fields are the sheep and cattle which provide the prime source of farm income. Grass is the predominant feature of the fields but some bottom land in the dales may be given over to arable. Harvests of cereals, roots and grass for silage provide valuable feedstuff for livestock over the winter.

Primarily, these dale farms are the country's breeding ground for sheep and cattle. The livestock is sold off for fattening or cross-breeding on the richer grasslands of lowland farms. Dairy cows can also be seen on some of the farms, and the modern bulk milk tankers have the unenvious task of negotiating the narrow daleside roads to reach them.

Many of the dale farms also rely on the heather moorland for part of their income. For generations the dale farms have had the rights to graze sheep on the open moor. Areas of moorland grazing (moor strays) are allocated to particular farms. The rights to moorland grazing are often essential to the economic viability of a farm, particularly where the farm holds relatively few fields of improved grassland in the dale.

Below: Amid a landscape of green fields, bracken hillsides and heather moors are the traditional farmsteads with their stone-built walls and red, clay pantiled roofs

Pages 62-3: Centuries-old, dry stone walls as seen here in Esk Dale, near Danby, provide the traditional field boundaries throughout the moorland dales. Placed at strategic points along the moorland roads are the cattle grids which prevent the sheep from leaving the open moor

THE HARDY SWALEDALE

Moorland sheep must obviously be of a hardy breed to withstand the rigours of the moorland winters. Swaledales, with their black faces and white noses, are the most favoured breed. Both sexes are horned, the ewes have single curved horns but the tups have horns with up to triple curves.

BURNING THE MOORS

Regulations allow controlled burning to take place each year during the period between late autumn and the following early spring, without a licence. During this time of year the birds are not nesting and the peat is mostly damp and therefore unlikely to be set on fire. When burning is in progress, great plumes of smoke can be seen rising above the skyline of the moors.

Above: Swaledales – although sheep have almost no road sense, they do have an innate sense of territory belonging to their own particular flock
Opposite: Patches of old heather are burned to encourage fresh growth. This is an essential part of moorland management for sheep and grouse

On any journey across the moors, the visitor will almost certainly see sheep grazing on the heather. The sheep don't have any road sense and a number of them are killed every year on the open roads. Motorists are always asked to drive carefully and in particular when there are young lambs about. Road deaths of young lambs are a financial disaster to the farmer and losses each year can amount to up to 10 per cent of a particular flock. That is why some stretches of the moorland roads have been fenced. There is some regret in this perceived 'taming' of the moorland roads, but fast-moving traffic and sheep just do not mix. Sheep do however have one notable sense – the sense of territory.

Each flock has a knowledge of its own particular grazing territory, referred to as a stray or 'heft'. They are what the farmer says 'heafed' to their home moor. This sense is passed on from the ewes to their lambs through each generation.

Despite that innate sense of their own territory, moorland sheep also carry some means of identification to show that they belong to their individual flocks. A long-established system of sheep marks is used which includes paint, horn marks and ear clippings.

Agricultural use of the moor is not reserved exclusively for sheep rearing. It is shared with grouse shooting as a means of gaining some financial return from the vast expanse of heather. From a cursory glance, there appears to be almost no variation in the moorland vegetation, but a closer look reveals some differences. There may be patches of dark peatland stripped of any vegetation with a scattering of grey twisted twigs. Elsewhere, tinges of green appear where young shoots of heather indicate signs of regrowth. In old age, stands of heather are straggly and knee-high. Throughout the moorland plateau, there is a mosaic of different heights of heather. This pattern is the result of the deliberate and systematic burning of the moor.

The aim of the burning by gamekeepers is to provide a variety of habitats for the grouse. Patches of deep heather are favoured for roosting and nesting, where the grouse are well hidden. They blend in so well with the background that they are almost impossible to observe on the ground. Until they gain flight, the young chicks also need a nearby area of short heather on which to feed. The moorland sheep obviously also benefit from the young shoots of heather which provide a more nutritious feed.

Deliberate burning of moorland areas is referred to as 'controlled' burning and is done on a rotational system which can vary from seven to fifteen or more years. 'Swiddens' or 'swizzens' is the local term for the burnt patches.

The whole purpose is simply to burn off the old woody heather and encourage young shoots to come up from the roots. It is important not to let the fire burn with an intensity that would destroy the heather roots and the peat. That is the theory, but fire is an unpredictable phenomenon. Thankfully, there are few occasions when controlled burning becomes out of control. When this happens the farmers and gamekeepers need the assistance of the Fire Service and sometimes additional volunteers.

Apart from the burning, the only other management of the moor has been drainage. In earlier times there was a view that if rainwater was drained more speedily off the moor, the drier land conditions would be beneficial for the grouse. Consequently certain areas of moor were cut with long lines of drainage channels, known as grips. Some of the grips are quite deep and sadly, the consequences of gripping the moor were not properly understood. The quickened run-off of rainwater has added to the potential for flooding on lower ground during periods of heavy rain. In addition, the deep grips are a hazard to grouse chicks, sheep and humans. Being half-hidden by vegetation, the drainage channels are a danger to the unwary.

From the 1850s onwards, a surge of interest in grouse shooting gave landowners a fresh financial incentive for their moorland wilderness. Jobs were provided for gamekeepers and during the shooting season (12 August to 10 December) day work was available for beaters, loaders and other ancillary staff. Today there are about thirty gamekeepers in the moors, assisted by many casual workers on moorland management and on shooting days. Only rarely are visitors likely to see a shoot in progress with the beaters walking in line to raise the birds in flight towards the guns. Carefully camouflaged as part of the moorland landscape are lines of shooting butts which provide the stations for the shooters.

The North York Moors contain the largest extent of heather moorland in England and Wales. However, we have already seen that it is very much a managed landscape. Rotational burning of the moorland produces pure stands of heather in a variety of stages of growth. Providing that the economics of moor-

GROUSE BUTTS

The traditional shooting butts are fine pieces of workmanship. A generally oblong-shaped structure is built with a drystone wall and narrow entrance. The wall is mounded over on the outside with peat and heather. Within each roofless compound there is space for a shooter and a loader. On some moors you may see a line of fencing panels. These are simply a cheap, modern alternative to the shooting butts.

land sheep farming and grouse shooting are viable, traditional maintenance of the heather will continue. Any decline in these activities will inevitably result in a deterioration of the heather. In that situation, a mixed heathland scrub would gradually be established. If society wants the countryside, including the moorland, to survive and adapt to the continuing pressure of change, then some financial support is necessary.

Support comes in the form of various grants and subsidies from the Ministry of Agriculture, Fisheries and Food (MAFF), the European Union and the North York Moors National Park Authority. Funds to encourage a range of moorland management work have been distributed under a Moorland Regeneration Programme which is co-ordinated by the National Park Authority. The primary aim has been to improve the quality of the moorland and to improve the health of the sheep and grouse.

Apart from improvement grants, central to the financial survival of almost all hill farmers, are the subsidies that they receive for their livestock. Hill farmers receive a payment from the Government for each sheep they send to market. Without this upland sheep subsidy there would be no sheep on the moor. A steady decline in the prices paid for sheep and cattle at livestock markets simply means that farmers' dependence on subsidies increases. In almost every aspect there is a decline in hill farming and the long-term future is uncertain. Like elsewhere, there has been some amalgamation of the daleside farms, but they are still essentially family-run farms with maybe one or two farm workers.

Coming down off the moor there is generally a fringe of bracken around the topmost edges of the dales. Sometimes it will colonise a substantial area of hillside and encroach onto the moorland. Bracken spreads by its strong underground rhizomes and can smother all other vegetation. There is no formal policy to totally eradicate the bracken from the landscape – it would be extremely expensive and uneconomic to do so. Nevertheless it does need to be controlled. In times past, dales farmers used to cut bracken and use it as winter bedding for their cattle, and this may have had some local effect in reducing the spread of bracken. Today, the most cost-effective way of controlling bracken is by machine crusher or by using helicopters for aerial spraying with herbicides. Happily there are programmes of bracken control that are promoted and grant-aided by the National Park Authority.

Below the fringe of bracken is the patchwork of improved fields bordered by miles of drystone walls. As the description infers, these are walls that are built 'dry', that is without any binding material such as mortar.

There is richer farmland on the southern and coastal edges of the North York Moors, dictated by the geology and the soils of these regions. Across the Tabular Hills and the Hambleton Hills there are some 430 working farms which include livestock, arable and mixed farms. Well-drained, light soils are found on the limestone and calcareous grit bedrock of the Tabular and Hambleton Hills. The main arable crops are barley, wheat, oilseed rape, potatoes and sugar beet. Intensive production of pigs and poultry have also been established at a few locations. Many drystone walls in these farmlands have decayed over the years and been replaced with posts and fencing. The walls were built of local limestone which is often relatively soft. As a result, the walls fall victim to the years of weathering, and eventually crumble into disrepair.

Along the length of the coastal region there is another belt of noticeably good farmland. The soils are based on layers of sands, clays, gravel and boulders which

WATCHING OVER THE WALLS

From the moorland heights you can look down into a dale and view the pattern of the centuries-old field boundaries. They are an integral part of the North York Moors landscape. In recent years there has been a revival in the skill of building and repairing stone walls. Over 350 miles (563km) of stone walls have been repaired under a scheme operated by the National Park Authority.

Opposite: The long shadows from the winter sun strengthen the pattern of the field boundaries. A sense of desolation creeps across the moorland landscape on dark days, reminding us of its former name of 'Blackamoor'

Left: The view from Spaunton Moor across Rosedale to Rosedale East shows the spread of improved land extending up the daleside. The impact of the twentieth-century conifer planting is seen on the high ground

Above: Little Fryup Dale: only a few farms are located in this small, peaceful dale. Little Fryup Beck, marked by the central line of trees, is a north-flowing tributary which joins with the River Esk near Danby

Pages 70-1: The valley of the Derwent provides good farmland with richly wooded hillsides. The hilltops of the surrounding Tabular Hills are extensively planted with conifer forests

were originally scoured from other regions. They were carried forward in a frozen mix within the base of advancing ice sheets along the coast. At the end of the Ice Age, the ice sheets melted and deposited the so-called 'boulder clay' on top of the bedrock. The boulder clay can be worked into good farmland and the coastal strip supports 226 working farms engaged in rearing lowland cattle and sheep, dairying and arable cultivation. Only in one small area near Ravenscar does the heather moorland come close to the North Sea cliffs.

During the past 4,000 years of human settlement in the North York Moors, there has been a story of continued destruction of woodland. It began during the Bronze Age with the clearance of mixed woodland on the upland plateau. In the dales and fringes of the moors it continued in response to a growing population and the various demands for agricultural land and timber for house construction, ship building, railways, coal mining and industry. By 1900, no more than 8 per cent of the land in the North York Moors was woodland.

When natural resources such as trees are taken without consideration for conservation, there is always a penalty to pay. It took World War I for the United Kingdom to realise how vulnerable and dependent on foreign imports of timber it had become. After the war, the Government set up the Forestry Commission in 1919 to plant trees and start a commercial forest enterprise. Even today, the UK imports 80 per cent of its timber requirement.

Left: A fine view of Bilsdale is seen looking northwards from the viewing platform in Newgate Bank car park
Above: On an exposed site near Ravenscar, this windmill once harnessed the power of the north-easterlies coming off the North Sea

QUOIT THE THING TO DO

Examples of traditional customs, games and pastimes are most likely to survive in the remoter dales. One centuries-old game which is still played in a few Esk Valley villages is quoits. A heavy iron ring (the quoit) is thrown a distance of some 25ft (7.6m). Skill and strength are needed to power the quoit through the air and hopefully land over or against a metal pin (the hob). During summer evenings the clang of metal against metal resounds when members of a local quoits league meet to do battle. Visitors may notice a collection of box-shaped covers that are spaced out on an area of village green. These are the quoits pitches, and underneath the covers are the pitches of clay that must be kept from drying out.

Opposite: Laurence Sterne, the eccentric vicar, author and humorist arrived in Coxwold in 1760. He lived in this fifteenth-century house which he named Shandy Hall

In 1920, the Forestry Commission purchased land at Dalby, near Thornton le Dale and began planting conifer woodlands the following year. The trend of centuries was reversed. About 15 per cent of the National Park is now used to grow timber commercially, and produces approximately 80,000 tonnes of timber a year. Forest Enterprise (an agency of the Forestry Commission) is responsible for the management of the state-owned forests. Although the primary goal is timber production, the forests of Dalby, Cropton and Wykeham now also offer extensive opportunities for walking, cycling, orienteering and horse riding.

There have been so many dramatic changes in our lifestyles during the twentieth century that it is almost surprising to find anything which remains to identify a region's culture and customs. Many aspects are remembered if not practised while others have passed into the realm of folk tales or legends which identify characters of the past.

The North York Moors has already been described as a cradle of Christianity in northern England. There are abundant reminders of the Christian tradition throughout the area, including seventh-century monastic sites, fragments of Anglo-Saxon age, Norman abbeys and churches, seventeeth-century Quaker meeting houses and burial grounds, eighteenth-century Methodist chapels and a nineteenth-century Roman Catholic abbey. Christian witness is also recorded for posterity in the list of revered saints, monks, a Roman Catholic martyr and the notable clergymen who led their congregations down through the ages.

Literature pays homage to Caedmon, a seventh-century monk of Whitby Abbey, as the Father of English Poetry and to the eighteenth-century vicar of Coxwold, Laurence Sterne, as the Father of the Modern English Novel. Another local clergyman, Canon John Christopher Atkinson, left us a valuable piece of local writing. In his *Forty Years in a Moorland Parish* he gives a fine insight into life in his parish of Danby during the latter half of the nineteenth century. But perhaps above all else, the world has been made aware of the moorland and dales through twentieth-century popular literature. James Herriot, the one-time vet-

erinary surgeon of nearby Thirsk, drew inspiration for his fictional tales from both the Yorkshire Dales and the North York Moors. Also placed firmly in the moors are the writings of the profilic local author, Peter N. Walker, whose police exploits of the 1950s are the basis of his *Constable* books published under the alias of Nicholas Rhea. These books were adapted by Yorkshire Television for the immensely popular *Heartbeat* series.

Agricultural shows are a common enough occurrence in all rural areas of England, and there are no less than ten local shows in the North York Moors. Each year in the village of Egton Bridge, contestants arrive with their produce for one of the area's highly competitive shows, but this is the only one of its kind still surviving in Yorkshire. The Egton Bridge Old Gooseberry Show has been held since 1800. Nurtured with all the patience, skill, secrecy and enthusiasm that the growers can muster, the gooseberries are judged by the single criteria of their weight. Records are made to be broken, and in August 1994 a new gooseberry named 'Goliath' was presented at the show. A single berry weighed in at 31 drams, 22 grains (almost 2oz).

Below: Anne Lawson at the Staithes Gift Shop keeps alive the tradition of the Staithes Bonnet
Bottom: Champion Brian Nellist tends his entries in preparation for the Egton Bridge Old Gooseberry Show

Such is the way of fashion that items of traditional dress have become both a rarity and a curiosity. A traditional outfit in rustic-coloured tweeds of plus fours, waistcoat and jacket along with brogues, long socks, shirt with collar and tie and headgear of a flat cap or deerstalker is still maintained as the proper clothing for grouse shooters and gamekeepers. One item of headdress, the Staithes bonnet, is highly distinctive and has just about survived from the nineteenth-century heydays of the fishing industry along the North Sea coast. Made out of nine pieces of linen or cotton, broadly flared at the sides with double-pleated front frill and double-thickness crown, the Staithes bonnet has not been entirely lost. It was a protective item of headgear but it was also an attractive garment. The bonnets must have enlivened the appearance of the fishermen's wives and daughters as they toiled at the messy job of preparing fish for market.

Thirty-eight days after Easter Sunday is the Eve of Ascension Day – the date of a ceremony that must be among the oldest observed customs in the country. The 'Planting of the Penny Hedge' has probably been carried out in Whitby for hundreds of years. At 9am on Ascension Eve, three gumbooted men stand on the mudflats of the upper harbour on the east side of the town. Sightseers gather to watch. Hazel stakes are hammered into the mud and branches are interwoven to make a small length of simple fencing. Then a horn is sounded and the hornblower shouts 'Out on ye, out on ye, out on ye'. The unique custom of Planting the Penny Hedge is completed for yet another year.

This ceremony is a penance for a murder said to have been committed over 800 years ago in 1159. While out hunting in the local woods, three noblemen chased a wild boar into a chapel near Sleights. The hermit monk tried to prevent a kill but was mortally wounded himself by the hunters. On his death bed the hermit asked the abbot of Whitby to give the noblemen a pardon. In return for their pardon the hermit placed upon them, and their successors, an annual penance of planting a 'hedge' on Whitby harbourside. The stakes and twigs for the hedge had to be cut with 'a knife of one penny price', hence the name. Failure to carry out the ceremony or failure of the hedge to

withstand three tides was to result in forfeiture of all lands owned by them or their successors. However, the penance would be cancelled for all time if high water flooded the mudflats and made it impossible to plant the hedge. As far as we know this situation never arose until 1981, when a freak high tide covered the harbourside to a depth of 8ft (2.4m). Nature finally released the centuries-old penance and ownership of the lands was no longer under threat. Nevertheless, the family members responsible for the hedge planting resolved that the tradition should not die and Whitby's Penny Hedge continues to be planted each Ascension Eve.

In an ever-increasingly technological world it seems that the future will inevitably see a continuing loss of our moorland culture and customs. But at least one reminder of that heritage is secure. A visit to the award-winning Ryedale Folk Museum at Hutton le Hole assures visitors that the story of everyday life in our moors and dales is being conserved for our enjoyment and understanding.

Above: Pondering over the ancient game of merrils at the Ryedale Folk Museum in Hutton le Hole
Pages 78-9: A panoramic prospect of Whitby from East Cliff, near Whitby Abbey

5 Recreation

When Charles Dickens journeyed through the North York Moors in 1844 he travelled on what he described as 'the quaint old railway along part of which passengers are hauled by a rope'. He was referring to the Whitby to Pickering railway and in particular to the steep incline between Beck Hole and Goathland. Opened in 1836, this railway was indeed 'quaint' to say the least. A single horse pulled a coach along the railway at 10 miles per hour and it took two-and-a-half hours to get from Whitby to Pickering. The system of hauling the carriages up the Beck Hole incline by rope was even stranger, and potentially deadlier – especially when the rope broke!

It is still possible to journey by rail from Pickering to Whitby, but the incline experience of the early days no longer exists. The best way of discovering what Dickens was writing about is to follow the route of the rail trail from Goathland to Grosmont. This route is described in a booklet published by the National Park Authority, which will guide you along the easy and delightful 3 1/2 mile (6km) walk. You can walk from Goathland to Grosmont and travel back in the comfort of the train.

Below: The sights and sounds of a steam railway are enjoyed by those who journey on the North Yorkshire Moors Railway. The line runs through the impressive valley of Newton Dale for the greater part of its route

ESK VALLEY LINE

Keeping close company with the River Esk is the Esk Valley Line (below) which tracks its way through the valley on its way to the coast at Whitby. This is a working railway in use throughout the year, taking children to school, people to work and shoppers to the towns of Middlesbrough and Whitby. But it is also a largely undiscovered gem for visitors to the National Park. You can hop on and off at eleven different stations to explore the valley, via a network of footpaths which link adjoining stations. A whole area of fascinating countryside can be explored without resort to a car.

Despite the axing of hundreds of miles of Britain's railway routes in the 1960s, there are still two railway routes along which you can travel through the National Park. These are the North Yorkshire Moors Railway (Pickering to Grosmont) and the Esk Valley Line (Middlesbrough to Whitby). The two railways have adjacent platforms at Grosmont, and this adds to the permutations for exploration of the Park by rail.

The steam train journey from Pickering to Grosmont is not to be missed and the scenery through Newton Dale is every bit as impressive as it was in Charles Dickens' day. Here is the chance to indulge in the sights and sounds of the days of steam railway. Sit back and enjoy the views and 'let the train take the strain'. The North Yorkshire Moors Railway operates steam trains from Pickering to Goathland and on to Grosmont. In addition to these main stations you can leave or join the train at Levisham Station and Newtondale Halt. From Newtondale Halt there are opportunities to explore the valley by using the series of walks and paths which lead through the forest to some spectacular viewpoints along the high cliffs.

In recent years we have become aware of our increasing dependence on the motor car and the consequent loss of public transport facilities. Pollution and congestion have caused us to think again – not only in relation to our towns and cities, but also in respect of our countryside. During the summer and at weekends in particular, there are many tourist honeypots in the North York Moors that buzz with too many cars. Some of our enjoyment of a peaceful countryside is inevitably sacrificed. So what can be done? It is a question which is continually being addressed by the National Park Authority.

Part of the solution for a cleaner, more peaceful National Park lies in the Moorsbus Network – the National Park's own coach service. The Moors Connections timetables provide all the information required to get out and about by bus or train throughout the Park. Copies of the annual timetable are available at Tourist Information Centres and Village Information Points.

Above left: There is a level crossing and station at Levisham on the railway route through Newton Dale

Above: The extensive ruins of the abbey lie adjacent to the houses and cottages sin the small village of Rievaulx

Below: The Cleveland Way long-distance trail closely follows the coastline from Saltburn to Filey. Sections of the coastal path can be linked to a number of circular walks in the National Park

There is no shortage of examples which demonstrate that the North York Moors meets one of the prime purposes of National Park designation, that is to promote the enjoyment of the Park by the public. Hopefully, the visitor's enjoyment will never be at the expense of the other prime purpose, conservation. It has been clear for many years that conservation of the landscape in National Parks must always take priority. It is the duty of the North York Moors National Park Authority to exercise wisdom in balancing the almost inevitable conflicts of interest.

WALKING

You cannot look at any corner of the North York Moors without being aware of its potential for recreation. An initial exploration of the Park will tell you that above all else this is a landscape made for walking. Many people have discovered the health, sanity and well-being that is regained through walking in the countryside. Whether you walk alone or in a group, a walk in the countryside is the perfect anti-dote to the stress, strains and pace of everyday living. The historian and National Park campaigner G.M. Trevelyan put it this way: 'I have two doctors, my left leg and my right. When body and mind are out of gear... I know that I shall only have to call in my doctors and I shall be well again'. For strollers and long-distance walkers, and everyone else in between, there are 1,400 miles (2,200km) of public rights of way to be discovered and enjoyed in the National Park. Encouraging the public use of our National Parks for recreation is one of the prime duties of the National Park Authorities. Thanks to the work carried out over many years by the Rangers and field staff of the Authority, the North York Moors has a network of footpaths and bridleways which is well sign-posted and provided with good stiles and gates. These days, a bewildering choice of books on country walks confronts the visitor. You could start by looking at the series of walks booklets and packs of leaflets published by the National Park Authority, or consider joining the company of fellow walkers on a guided walk listed among a host of activities published in the annual National Parks events leaflet.

Looking back at the history of recreation in the North York Moors, ready access to the countryside only became available to our urban population with the building of the railways during the latter half of the nineteenth century. Many Victorians had a zest for natural history and for those with time on their hands there was opportunity for countryside exploration and to pursue their interests, particularly in identifying wildflowers.

Two organisations which were set up during the 1930s are a gauge of the growing interest in country walking today. For many years this outdoor activity was referred to as hiking or rambling. The Youth Hostels Association was founded in 1930 and was quickly followed by the Ramblers' Association in 1935. Unlike some other parts of England, freedom to roam across open moorland has not been a major confrontational issue in the North York Moors, and there has always been a degree of tolerance. Access has never had the history of fierce clashes between walkers and moorland gamekeepers which characterised the Peak District in the 1920s and 30s. There will be a new right of access on foot to areas of mountain, moor, heath, down and common land which will affect virtually all parts of England and Wales.

One of the best-known walkers in the area at the beginning of the twentieth century was Alec Falconer, who was one of the founder members of the Middlesbrough Rambling Club. After the founding of the Youth Hostels Association in 1930, he helped to promote the idea of a long-distance holiday walk around the periphery of

THE VIGOROUS VICAR

It is doubtful if many of us will be able to match the 70,000 miles (112,650km) of walking that Canon Atkinson, vicar of Danby, estimated he completed during the ministry of his moorland parish between 1847 and 1900. Atkinson's country walking was undertaken in the course of his duties, walking from the vicarage to the church, visiting his scattered flock of parishioners and in pursuit of his interests in archaeology and natural history.

Below: The Cleveland Way descends Black Hambleton and follows an old road across Thimbleby Moor, en route for Osmotherley

the moors, with hostels all along the route. This was the conception of the 108-mile (173km) Cleveland Way, which runs between Helmsley, Saltburn-by-the Sea, Whitby, Scarborough to Filey. Almost forty years later, it received the official status of a designated long-distance path when in May 1969, an official opening ceremony at Helmsley Youth Hostel confirmed the Cleveland Way as England's second long-distance footpath (now National Trail). Sadly, Alec Falconer died a year before the opening of the Cleveland Way, but anyone who walks the route will find a memorial to his name. A stone seat on Cringle End at the edge of the Cleveland Hills provides a welcome rest, a splendid view and an appropriate commemoration to a fine walker. Over the years, eleven Youth Hostels were established in and around the moors. Of these, Boggle Hole (near Robin Hood's Bay), Helmsley, Lockton, Osmotherley, Scarborough and Whitby are still open.

A major impact on the walking scene in the moors appeared in 1959 with the publication of a book entitled *Lyke Wake Walk* written by a local farmer, Bill Cowley. This is a 40-mile (64km) crossing of the central heather moorland of the moors from the escarpment edge of the Cleveland Hills at Osmotherley to the North Sea coast at Ravenscar. As a challenge walk (to be walked within twenty-four hours) it gripped the imagination of many and became the most famous walk in the moors. During the 1960s and 70s, it was a favourite route for charity walks. Walkers arrived in large groups from all over the country, complete with their support parties who waited at strategic points along the way. Unfortunately the moorland peat was too fragile to withstand the passage of so many feet. Erosion resulted in the moorland equivalent of a motorway, in some parts up to 100yd (100m) in width. The National Park Authority gained initial co-operation in pleading for numbers to be reduced, and parties of more than ten are still requested not to use this route. Five thousand walkers a year is regarded as tolerable but there are signs that this number is currently being exceeded. Unlike earlier days, there are now plenty of alternative long-distance challenge routes in the moors.

Over the years, the Cleveland Way has become the prime long-distance walking route in the North York Moors. The National Park Authority noted its growing popularity, which became increasingly obvious during the 1980s. Every year, large numbers of walkers caused considerable erosion of the route, particularly along the moorland sections. Also along the coast path, the problem of coastal erosion made some sections difficult and dangerous. In 1989, the Cleveland Way Project was formed to undertake remedial work to the benefit of the walkers, wildlife and the landscape. Traditional path-building techniques which fit into the landscape have been used, including stone slabs and the age-old method of stone pitching.

Recreational opportunities in the countryside of the Park are not confined to country walking. People also take to the North York Moors on touring cycles, mountain bikes and horseback. They sail in boats and paddle in canoes on the water. Rock faces are climbed, rivers are fished and others take to the air in hang

THE CLEVELAND WAY

Virtually every area of countryside in Britain today has its long-distance walking route. In the North York Moors the prime attraction is the Cleveland Way National Trail (left). It is regarded as one of the finest long-distance walks with its range and variety of scenery and interests along the way. This is due largely to the fact that it combines both moorland and coastal sections of countryside with panoramic views, varied landscapes, ancient monuments and attractive villages.

Above: Adapted from a former shooting lodge (Danby Lodge) is the National Park Centre (The Moors Centre), near Danby village. The facilities at the Centre provide an excellent introduction to exploring the National Park

gliders and gliders. Wheelchair access is provided at the two National Park Centres, The Moors Centre (near Danby) and at Sutton Bank, and the National Park Authority has made the paths accessible to wheelchairs through Crow Wood at The Moors Centre, and also along the escarpment path at Sutton Bank.

MOTORING

When the Forestry Commission starting planting trees in the North York Moors in 1921, there was no conception that the public would ever be invited into the forests for recreation. The sole purpose was to grow trees for timber. During the following thirty years, foresters were decidedly suspicious of allowing anyone to wander through the plantations. However, a change of heart came in the 1950s and a programme of providing recreational opportunities began. A major step forward came in 1960 with the creation of the Dalby Forest Drive. The route used a tarmac road that had originally been made to provide access for vehicles involved in the search for oil and gas. The forest drive also gave the Commission an important additional source of income as it charged for public vehicles. Traffic gradually increased and a second route, the Newtondale Forest Drive, was created.

Apart from enjoying the scenic delights along the routes of the forest drives, there are plenty of opportunities to leave the car for a while at the tempting viewpoints, parking areas and picnic spots. A variety of walks are waymarked through the forests. Recreational opportunities within the forests are now the responsibility of Forest Enterprise. Facilities include routes for orienteering, horse riding and mountain bikes. Details are available from the Tourist Information Centres and at the Dalby Forest Visitor Centre at Low Dalby, located north of Thornton le Dale and near the start of the Forest Drive.

CYCLING

Many miles of country roads, bridleways and forest tracks in the North York Moors offer a great variety of routes for cyclists of all ages. For visitors who come to the Park without a cycle or mountain bike there is still the opportunity to enjoy riding through the Park on two wheels. There are ten outlets which hire bikes for full day and half-day outings in the Park. Maps, books and leaflets are available to ensure that you get some of the best bike-friendly routes around. You can soon be on your bike, equipped with a cycle map that describes a choice of six routes, designed for a range of abilities. A family cycle route around Sutton Bank involves everyone in finding clues and solving riddles.

RIDING

Holidays are often the time when many people sample outdoor activities for the first time. Experienced and not-so-experienced horse riders are catered for by most of the fourteen riding centres located in the area. Pony trekking along the quiet bridleways and tracks of the National Park is something that visitors remember with great pleasure.

FISHING

Anyone interested in fishing will find an excellent choice among the rivers, lakes and reservoirs located in and around the Park. Of particular interest is the River Esk, the only river in Yorkshire to support salmon and sea trout. It is also an important fishery for brown trout and grayling. There are areas for permit fishing along the Rivers Esk, Derwent and Rye and their tributaries.

Lakes and reservoirs are available for fishing at eight locations and the largest stretch of water in the Park is at Scaling Dam, alongside the A171 Guisborough to Whitby road. On the nearby Lockwood Beck Reservoir where rowing boats are hired for fishing purposes only, the record for a rainbow trout stands at 14lb (6.35kg). Some locations also have special facilities for the disabled angler. Those who are attracted by the North Sea for a spot of fishing will find that the local fishermen at Staithes, Whitby and Scarborough offer boat fishing. Permits and a current rod licence are of course required to fish all the rivers and inland waters in the Park.

Top: A variety of routes have been specially devised for an exploration of the Sutton Bank area by cycle
Above: One of the most popular stopping points in the National Park is at Sutton Bank. The National Park Centre offers information, exhibitions, bookshop, picnic areas, tearoom and toilets

WATERSPORTS

Some inland areas of water are available for dinghy sailing, canoeing and windsurfing. Details are available on hire and tuition facilities at Scaling Dam and Wykeham Lakes. At several locations along the coast, there are facilities for offshore sailing. Remember that advice on weather conditions for offshore sailing is readily available from HM Coastguard at Whitby and the Humber. For a more leisurely pastime there are rowing boats for hire on the River Esk at Ruswarp.

CLIMBING

Many generations of rock climbers have met the challenges of the rock outcrops of the North York Moors. As far as is known, the first rock climber to explore the moors was E.E. Roberts who, in 1906, ventured on to the prominent rocks known as The Wainstones. These rocky pinnacles form part of the north-facing escarpment

edge of the Cleveland Hills some 4 miles (6km) southeast of Stokesley. There is a popular walk to the Wainstones from the car park at Clay Bank, and the Cleveland Way National Trail follows a narrow path between the jumble of boulders and bare rock outcrops. With the exception of a few outcrops near Danby and Peak Scar near Hawnby, the rock-climbing activity in the Park is virtually confined to the sandstone rocks along the escarpment edges of the Cleveland Hills. The one major exception is Whitestone Cliff near Sutton Bank where beds of limestone and calcareous grits provide distinct bedding planes, steep vertical cracks, horizontal ledges and overhangs.

AIRSPORTS

One of the attractions often seen at Sutton Bank is the spectacle of the gliders as they circle effortlessly in the skies above. If you wish to experience the world of wind-borne flight then you can contact the clubhouse of the Yorkshire Gliding Club at the nearby airfield. You can look at the North York Moors from a lofty viewpoint with air experience flights, trial flights, lessons and holiday courses.

An up-to-date guide on recreational opportunities in and around the Park is published annually in the North York Moors National Park Authority's visitor newspaper. This is on sale in the Tourist Information Centres, Village Information Points and in many of the shops around the Park.

Above: The rocky outcrop at The Wainstones, south of Great Broughton, is one of the few locations in the North York Moors that offers some sport to rock climbers
Opposite: Although lying outside the National Park boundary, Scarborough is a popular venue for visitors to the North York Moors

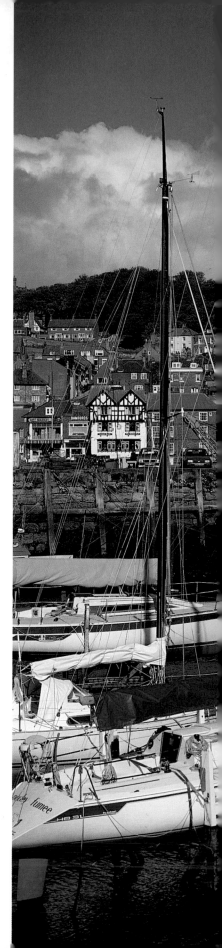

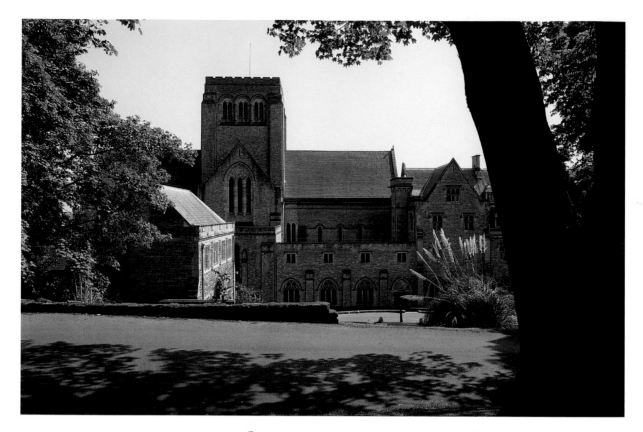

6 Exploring the Park

*Above: Ampleforth Abbey –
Benedictine monks settled in
Ampleforth in 1802. Six years later
they started a school that has
become the world-famous
Ampleforth College*

AMPLEFORTH

The old part of Ampleforth (pop 1,340) sits tight against the warm, south-facing slope of the Hambleton Hills. A narrow driveway leads off the main street to the Roman Catholic church of Our Lady and St Benedict, built in 1907. In the church-yard is an oak cross, a memorial to those lost in World War I, carved by Robert Thompson who was to become famous as the Mouseman of Kilburn.

On the eastern outskirts of the village are the Benedictine Ampleforth Abbey, the largest monastic foundation in the country, and Ampleforth College. Visitors are welcome. Open to the public are the abbey church, the concourse of the central building, the grounds, the apple orchard and some of the facilities of the St Alban Sports Centre. The present abbey church was opened in 1961 and its oak pews were also made in the Kilburn workshops of Robert Thompson. A rare medieval high altar rescued from the ruins of nearby Byland Abbey is preserved in the crypt of St Benet's chapel.

BECK HOLE

Beck Hole is a picturesque hamlet where the Eller Beck emerges from a steep-sided gorge and splashes over a rocky bed. Approaches by car down the steep, narrow roads are best avoided during the main visitor season as informal parking is extremely limited. However, Beck Hole can be reached easily by a pleasant stroll from the village of Goathland. Note that the pub sign at the Birch Hall Inn, a scene of the Eller Beck, was painted on sheet metal by Sir Algernon Newton, a member of the Royal Academy and an accomplished Victorian oil painter, who lived for a time in the village.

BOTTON HALL (BOTTON VILLAGE)

A minor road between Grosmont and Ainthorpe leads into Danby Dale and eventually reaches Botton Hall. This is the centre of a community for adults with special needs and is run on a largely self-sufficient basis by the Camphill Village Trust. Visitors are welcome at Botton Hall where there is a coffee shop, bookshop and gift shop with craft, bakery and creamery products.

BYLAND ABBEY

Situated between the villages of Coxwold and Wass, the ruins of Byland Abbey are a haunting spectacle, with a huge broken circular window at the west end. This great rose window, 26ft (8m) in diameter, was the dominant feature of the church. At the time the abbey church was built in the twelfth century (1177-97), it was the largest Cistercian church in Britain. Byland is renowned for its magnificent series of tiled floors. They date from the thirteenth century when the church was repaved, and much of this paving still survives. Although the glaze is worn, the intricate geometrical patterns are still intact.

Below: The ruin of a great circular window at the west end of Byland Abbey church is an imposing spectacle – especially by moonlight
Bottom: High on the hilltop at the north end of of the village of Coxwold is the unmistakable octagonal clock tower of the parish church

COXWOLD

Coxwold (pop 190) is a charming village which spreads over two facing hillsides leading steeply to a cross-roads in the dip. A wide main street is edged with trim greens and cobbles. There are substantial properties, cosy cottages, quaint almshouses and an inviting pub.

Dominating the village scene is the hilltop church with its unmistakable octagonal tower. Laurence Sterne was the eccentric vicar here for eight years (1760-68) and his inscribed headstone is in the churchyard. His vicarage which he aptly called Shandy Hall has a huge and very distinctive, leaning chimney. Shandy means 'odd' and visitors to the house will soon appreciate Sterne's equally eccentric house. He became a celebrated novelist and Shandy Hall is preserved to record the life and work of this acclaimed Father of the English Novel.

A quarter of a mile from Coxwold is Newburgh Priory. Originally an Augustinian Priory built in 1145, the priory was closed during the dissolution of monasteries in the sixteenth century. It was then turned into a magnificent Elizabethan country house set in beautiful grounds and has a splendid water garden. A sealed tomb within the house is said to contain the body of Oliver Cromwell.

DANBY

Most visitors to Danby (pop with Castleton, 1,560) will want to call at the National Park Centre – known as The Moors Centre, set in beautiful surroundings, just to the east of the village. The Moors Centre is the best place to discover what to see and do in the National Park. It offers some interesting interpretive exhibitions, an excellent bookshop and a range of events and activities. Outside there are pleasant picnic areas, a wildflower garden and paths through Crow Wood. Wheelchair

Above: Canon John C. Atkinson was vicar of Danby for fifty-three years (1847-1900). Curiously, the church is located at an isolated site more than a mile south of the village

access is available to the centre, tearoom, toilets and the Crow Wood paths.

Danby has the only remaining watermill working on the River Esk and the 350-year-old mill is open to the public. From Danby you can take the road through Ainthorpe and turn off along the minor road along Danby Dale to reach Botton Hall (qv).

EGTON BRIDGE

Egton Bridge (pop 490) is a small village with a remarkable church. Its houses, built on both sides of the River Esk, are linked by a double set of stepping stones and a fine stone bridge. Floods in 1930 largely destroyed the centuries-old stone bridge and it was replaced in 1931 by a steel structure. Nationwide interest was created in 1992 when the county council demolished the steel structure and began the building of a stone bridge, exact in every detail to the original three-span bridge of 1758. The new bridge was opened in February 1994.

St Hedda's Roman Catholic Church is of surprising size for such a small country parish. Inside there are even greater surprises, including a roof painted blue with golden stars and a showy altar made in Munich in about 1867. There is also a shrine to the martyred priest Nicholas Postgate who at the age of eighty was hanged, drawn and quartered at York in 1679. He was put to death because he baptised a child into the Catholic faith, which was illegal at the time.

The Egton Bridge Old Gooseberry Show is an annual event attracting gooseberry growers from far and wide. This contest is held on the first Tuesday in August in St Hedda's schoolroom. Founded in 1800, the show is now one of just nine left in the country devoted to this humble berry.

FARNDALE

The valley of Farndale (pop 180) is famous for the display of wild daffodils. Thousands of visitors come each April to walk the 3 miles (5km) from Low Mill to Church Houses along the river, enjoying the colourful scene. You should allow about two hours for the return walk. A Moorsbus service operates along the routes into Farndale during the daffodil season. Information on the bus services and on the flowering season is available from the local Tourist Information Centres.

GILLAMOOR

Leaving Gillamoor (pop 153) in the direction of Farndale, motorists will find a stunning panorama near the church known as Surprise View. The view extends across the valley of Farndale to the heather and bracken landscape of Spaunton Moor. St Aidan's Church, originally built in the twelfth century, was reconstructed single-handedly in 1802 by local stonemason James Smith. The church still has some screen fragments from its original building. Opposite the Methodist Church, an unusual and complex sundial stands by the pavement edge. It was erected in 1802 under the direction of the local schoolmaster, John Russell.

GLAISDALE

Glaisdale (pop 1,040) is a sprawling village of steeply terraced grey cottages built during the nineteenth century for local iron workers. The most popular stopping point is outside the village at Beggar's Bridge. This is a sturdy, single-arched bridge

Opposite below: St Hedda's church, Egton Bridge: the imposing Roman Catholic church has the 'Mysteries of the Rosary' depicted on an exterior wall
Below: A much-photographed location is the old packhorse bridge, Beggar's Bridge, over the River Esk at Glaisdale. Its romantic story lingers on

*Above: Mallyan Spout, Goathland –
not many visitors will have seen the
famous 'spout' of water transformed
into an ice sculpture*

*Opposite above: A landmark along
the skyline of the Cleveland Hills is
the monument on Easby Moor
erected in 1827 to the memory of
Captain James Cook. He went to
school in the nearby village of Great
Ayton*

*Opposite below: The night sky,
emblazoned by the lights of Teesside, emphasises the craggy outline
of Roseberry Topping. Light pollution
from many sources is an increasing
intrusion into the rural blackness of
the moorland night*

spanning the River Esk. Despite the nearby criss-cross of modern road and rail bridges there is a certain dignity, peace and
romance to be found here. A local youth, Tom Ferris, loved a girl
on the opposite side of the river and had to wade across each
time to go courting. The girl's father refused marriage because
Tom was 'as poor as a beggar', so Tom set out to sea from
Whitby, returned with a fortune and claimed his bride. As a witness of his love, he built the bridge to provide a dry passage over
the river for future generations. His initials are inscribed on the
bridge for all to see.

GOATHLAND

Goathland (pop 460) lies at a healthy 500ft (152m) above sea-
level in a broad triangular oasis of green farmland in a
surrounding landscape of heather moorland. Goathland became
a focus of national interest as the setting for 'Aidensfield' in the
successful *Heartbeat* drama series on ITV. A Goathland
Exhibition Centre displays aspects of village history and an
exclusive 'Heartbeat Collection'. Steam trains stop at the village
station en route to either Grosmont or Pickering.

There are some fine walks to be enjoyed from Goathland. A
well-used path leads to the waterfall called Mallyan Spout, where
a 'spout' of water plunges down a 70ft (21m) sheer rock face (visitors need to be
active enough to step through a boulder-strewn section of the valley to reach it).
An easy stroll follows the route of the 'Rail Trail' to Grosmont and you can return
by steam railway.

On the western outskirts of the village along the Egton Bridge road there is a
minor road signed to the Roman Road. This is on Wheeldale Moor and consists
of about a mile (2km) of rough roadway laid with flat stones. Although it has long
been considered as the best-preserved section of Roman road in Britain, its origin
is now regarded as uncertain. The roadway is locally referred to as Wade's
Causeway.

GREAT AYTON

Great Ayton (pop 4,660) is a much-loved village which keeps its treasures hidden away quietly from the main road. There are two spacious greens and part
of the village is bordered by the tumbling waters of the River Leven.
Associations with the world-famous Captain Cook are very much in evidence.
When the Cook family moved to Great Ayton in 1736, the young James Cook
went to school in the little schoolroom which is now the Captain Cook
Schoolroom Museum. The site of the Cook family cottage in Bridge Street is
marked with a granite memorial. In 1934, the cottage was dismantled, shipped
to Australia and rebuilt in Melbourne. In the graveyard of All Saints parish
church are the graves of Cook's mother, Grace Cook, and five of his sisters and
brothers. On Easby Moor above Great Ayton is the Cook Monument erected
in 1827. There is a walk to the monument from Gribdale Gate (take the road
leading past Great Ayton station).

Just one mile (2km) northeast of Great Ayton is the unmistakable hilltop of
Roseberry Topping. This can be climbed from the roadside car park at Newton-
under-Roseberry or included in a circular walk from Gribdale Gate.

Above: A glimpse of Hackness Hall
Opposite: Parts of the twelfth-
century church at Helmsley still
survive in the main doorway and
chancel arch. Victorian enthusiasm
for the 'restoration' of churches
resulted in a major rebuilding here
in 1866-69
Opposite below: Hutton le Hole is a
picturesque village with traditional
stone-built cottages, a large green
with a stream flowing through, and
was destined to be a popular place
for visitors

GROSMONT

Trains are the prime interest for visitors to Grosmont (pop 370). Ever since the reopening of the railway from Pickering to Grosmont in 1973, the village of Grosmont has flourished as the northern terminus for the North Yorkshire Moors Railway. A short stroll from the station is the locomotive repair shed where visitors can see work in progress from the viewing platform. Grosmont also has a platform for the Esk Valley Railway Line and visitors can continue a train journey from here to the coast at Whitby.

HACKNESS

Sheltered against the steeply rising slopes of the Hackness Hills, Hackness (pop 140) enjoys a sunny position overlooking the Derwent valley. The village lies at a short distance from the church, school and Hackness Hall. There are a few tempting glimpses of the great Georgian mansion house, its grounds and lake, but the house is not open to the public. Worthy of exploration are the numerous tributary dales that cut into the hills. Allowing for some steep climbs, this is good walking country.

St Peter's church has a noteworthy history and inside there are some items of interest. In the seventh century, St Hilda of Whitby Abbey sent a small group of nuns across the moors to establish a nunnery here. Peace reigned for almost 200 years until the Danes destroyed the nunnery in 869. A link with the past are the two fragments from a rare, early Anglian cross which contain inscriptions to an abbess at the nunnery. Also in the church is an alabaster tablet to Lady Margaret Hoby, who is recorded as the first woman diarist. She died in 1633 and her diary is held in the British Museum.

HELMSLEY

Hemlsley (pop 1,530; market day, Friday) is surely the most popular market town in Yorkshire, and it caters for tourists at all times of the year. First impressions are gained from the market place with its ancient market cross, pinnacled monument with statue, imposing town hall and the Black Swan Hotel, which incorporates a delightful sixteenth-century half-timbered house. Visitors have a choice of interest including the parish church, Helmsley Walled Garden, Helmsley Castle, and the fine country mansion known as Duncombe Park.

For 500 years, Helmsley Castle was the well-fortified home of the lord of the manor. It was 'slighted' by cannon-fire in 1644 during the English Civil War. The Parliamentarians did however spare the domestic buildings. Some interior fittings of the Tudor period survive. In 1713, the lord of the manor moved his place of residence from the castle to a newly built mansion house, Duncombe Park, on the edge of the town. A 5-acre walled garden, adjacent to the castle, has been restored and provides a secluded corner. Within the parish church are some very unusual nineteenth-century wall paintings and glass windows depicting the religious history of the area.

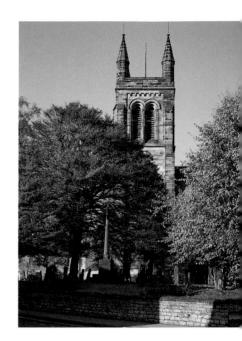

HUTTON LE HOLE

A showpiece village (pop 170) with attractive stone-built houses and a fast-moving moorland stream running through a pillowy village green. The prime attraction here is the Ryedale Folk Museum, Yorkshire's leading open-air museum which tells the story of 4,000 years of history in the area. Thirteen historic buildings reveal the story of everyday life with a sense of reality never captured in a history book. Special events are run during the year.

KILBURN

The fame of an oak-carved mouse brings visitors from all over the world to the workshops of Robert Thompson at Kilburn (pop 210). All the 'Mouseman' furniture has a hand-carved mouse somewhere on it. In addition to the showroom there is a Mouseman Visitor Centre. This tells the story of the one-time village wheelwright who became a world-renowned craftsman.

The giant turf-cut figure of the Kilburn White Horse stands on the hillside near the village. There is a pleasant walk along the escarpment edge from Sutton Bank to the White Horse.

KIRKBYMOORSIDE

Kirkbymoorside (pop 2,750; market day, Werdnesday) is a traditional market town with a wide range of services. Note the Black Swan Inn, with its timber-framed porch on shaped posts, dated 1634.

LASTINGHAM

Within the unusual parish church of Lastingham, which originates from an uncompleted monastic church, is a set of stone steps which lead you down to an unforgettable experience. In the damp, secluded stillness of a low, stone encompassed crypt, you are transported back to the eleventh century. Lastingham church, with its ancient crypt, is not to be missed.

LEALHOLM

A popular place for a picnic where the village green stretches down to the banks of the Esk. There is a landscaped shrub nursery at Poets Cottage. Upstream from the bridge is a set of stepping stones.

Above left: The village of Kilburn - famous for the 'Mouseman' furniture
Left: Lealholm
Opposite: St Mary's church, Lastingham, transports visitors back to the eleventh century when it was part-built as a monastery church. It has the finest example in England of a Norman crypt

LOW DALBY

Low Dalby is a village on the Dalby Forest Drive, north of Thornton le Dale. Facilities at Low Dalby include car park, toilets and visitor centre. Along the 9-mile (14km) forest drive between Thornton le Dale and Hackness there are forest walks, viewpoints, picnic spots and toilets.

NORTH YORKSHIRE MOORS RAILWAY

There are three main stations (Pickering, Goathland and Grosmont) along the 18 miles (29km) of the North Yorkshire Moors Railway. Steam-hauled trains operate on a daily service during the season. The route includes the scenic splendour of Newtondale, where you can use Levisham Station and Newtondale Halt to stop off and enjoy walks through the valley.

OSMOTHERLEY

Best known perhaps as the western terminus of the Lyke Wake Walk, Osmotherley (pop. 620) has always been a popular village with visitors and a good centre for country walks. There is a half-hour stroll from the village, via Rueberry Lane, to the Lady Chapel. This was a secret place of pilgrimage during the period of Roman Catholic persecution in the seventeenth century.

Mount Grace Priory is reached via the A19 about one mile (2km) north of the turn off for Osmotherley. A fully restored and furnished monk's cell is on display and an exhibition is housed in a fine seventeenth-century mansion house which was the original priory's guesthouse. This is England's best preserved example of a Carthusian priory.

PICKERING

Pickering (pop 6,590; market day, Monday) is a busy market town with a number of interests for visitors including the North Yorkshire Moors Railway Station, Pickering Castle, Beck Isle Museum of Rural Life and the parish church. The medieval period is reflected in the castle with its impressive mound and in the wall paintings of the parish church. Bygones of an earlier age are packed into the Beck Isle Museum and the age of steam is relived on the railway from Pickering to Grosmont.

RAVENSCAR

There are stunning views across the windswept cliffs over Robin Hood's Bay from the cliff-top village of Ravenscar (pop 330). An exhibition is housed in the National Trust Coastal Centre and a short walk takes you to the remains of the Peak Alum Works.

RIEVAULX

Rievaulx Abbey lies alongside the village while Rievaulx Terrace and Temples are reached directly off the Helmsley-Stokesley road. Set against a backcloth of wooded hillsides, the monastic ruins are an impressive sight. Here is one of England's largest and finest Cistercian abbeys. High on the hillside is a piece of eighteenth-century landscaping with a lawn terrace and two mock Greek temples. From the terrace there are fine views of the abbey ruins. In the Ionic Temple everything is set ready for an elaborate banquet.

Opposite above: Steam up and ready for the journey from Pickering to Grosmont on the North Yorkshire Moors Railway

Opposite below: The founder of Methodism, John Wesley, stood on the low stone table to preach during his many visits to Osmotherley. Butter was once sold from the table on market days

Above: Church of St Peter & St Paul, Pickering – the parish church has one of the most complete series of church wall paintings in England. The paintings date from the fifteenth century and tell their stories with intense images

Pages 102–3: The place where land meets sea often presents an air of mystery, romance and exhilaration. The scene at Robin Hood's Bay captures many such emotions

ROBIN HOOD'S BAY

This coastal village (pop 1,620) involves a steep walk down the main street to reach the rocky shoreline. By the end of the lower car park, before descending the bank, read the story of a remarkable lifeboat rescue in 1881. Intriguing alleyways thread their way between tightly-packed houses. There is a small local museum and the village itself gives a real sense of history. Alongside the slipway to the beach is the Old Coastguard Station – the site of a reconstruction of the original eighteenth-century building. This joint venture by the National Trust and the National Park Authority opened for visitors in 2000.

ROSEDALE ABBEY

There never was an abbey at Rosedale – just a small Cistercian nunnery. All that is left is the forlorn remnant of a belfry with part of a stone spiral staircase, behind the village church. The village became a frenzied frontier town in the nineteenth century, when ironstone was discovered in the dale. Rosedale Abbey is a popular tourist destination and there are a number of short walks in the area.

Below: The tranquil valley of Rosedale was transformed in the nineteenth century, with the discovery of ironstone, into a noisy, industrial valley. Today, the mining has all gone and the village of Rosedale Abbey is a popular tourist destination

RUNSWICK

Generally referred to as Runswick Bay, Runswick (pop with Staithes, 2,280) consists of a maze of cottages with miniature gardens huddled close to each other and to the steep-sided cliff. At the northern end of the seafront is the Thatched Cottage – the only remaining thatched house on the Yorkshire coast. Picturesque and fringed with golden sand, Runswick Bay is now largely a holiday village.

STAITHES

Staithes is a picture-postcard fishing village which attracts many visitors. It occupies a cliff-edge location, with houses and cottages crammed in on either side of a steep main street leading down to the harbour. James Cook, later Captain, served as an assistant in a harbour front shop in 1745-6. There is a Staithes Heritage Centre in a converted chapel in the High Street.

SUTTON BANK

One of the best known viewpoints in the Park. The Sutton Bank National Park Centre is here and there is an exciting interpretive exhibition and a full range of National Park publications in the bookshop. Wheelchair access is available to the centre, tearoom and toilets. Walks from Sutton Bank include the popular route to the Kilburn White Horse and the escarpment path is also suitable for wheelchairs. Wheelchair loan is available during the summer (check at the Centre).

Above: Fishing boats at Staithes find shelter in the narrow inlet of Staithes Beck. The inlet is bordered on the west side by the towering backdrop of Cowbar Nab

Below: Thatched cottages always make a pretty picture, and particularly so at Thornton le Dale alongside the clear, sparkling stream that runs through the village

THORNTON LE DALE

Thornton le Dale (pop 1,830) is a busy tourist village. The entrance to the large car park is located along the Malton road, and between the car park and the village is a large pond with resident ducks. A roadside stream adds to the charm of the village.

WHITBY

Whitby (pop 13,920; market day, Saturday) is a seaside town built along both sides of the River Esk with a fine harbour, beach and a variety of entertainments (right). The gaunt ruins of Whitby Abbey dominate the view of the East Cliff, and crowds jostle along the ancient streets of the East Side where the 199 steps lead up to St Mary's Church and the Abbey. Displays of Whitby's heritage can be seen at the Pannett Park Museum and Art Gallery, Whitby Archives, and the Captain Cook Memorial Museum.

Above: The seaside town of Whitby
Opposite: From almost any point in Whitby, the eye is drawn to the East Cliff and the windswept ruins of the thirteenth-century abbey perched on the cliff top

Information

USEFUL ADDRESSES

Association of National Park
  Authorities
Ponsford House
Moretonhampstead
Devon TQ13 8NL
Tel: 01647 440245

Brigantia Economic Development
  Centre
North Yorkshire County Council
County Hall
Northallerton DL7 8AH
Tel: 01609 5322271

Tees Valley Wildlife Trust
Bellamy Pavilion
Kirkleatham Old Hall
Redcar TS1O 5NW
Tel: 01642 759900

Council for National Parks
246 Lavender Hill
London SW11 1LJ
Tel: 020 7976 6433

Countryside Agency
John Dower House
Crescent Place
Cheltenham GL50 3RA
Tel: 01242 5213181

Countryside Agency
Yorkshire Regional Office
2nd Floor
Victoria Wharf Embankment 1V
Sovereign Street
Leeds LS1 4BA
Tel: 0113 246 9222

English Heritage (Northern
  Region)
Bessie Surtees House
41-44 Sandhill
Newcastle-upon-Tyne NE1 3JF
Tel: 0191 261 1585

English Nature (local office)
Genesis Building 1, Science Park
University Road
Heslington
York YO1O 5ZQ
Tel: 01904 435500

Forestry Commission
231 Corstorphine Road
Edinburgh EH12 7AT
Tel: 0131 334 0303

Forest Enterprise
(North York Moors Forest District)
Outgang Road
Pickering YO18 7EL
Tel: 01751 472771

National Trust
Yorkshire Regional Offices
Goddards
27 Tadcaster Road
Dringhouses
York YO2 2QG
Tel: 01904 702021

North Yorkshire Moors Association
Hon Sec Mr P.J.E. Woods
Rosedale Intake
Danby, Whitby
North Yorkshire YO21 2LX

North York Moors National Park
  Authority
The Old Vicarage
Bondgate
Helmsley
York YO62 5BP
Tel: 01439 770657
E-mail: info@northyork-npa.gov.uk
Website: www.northyorkmoors-
  npa.gov.uk

Royal Society for the Protection of
  Birds (local office)
4 Benton Terrace
Sandyford Road

Newcastle-upon-Tyne NE2 1QU
Tel: 0191 281 3366

Ryedale Natural History Society
Mr Jim Pewtress
Hammerton House
31 Piercy End
Kirkbymoorside
York YO62 6DQ
Tel: 01751 431001

Scarborough Field Naturalists'
  Society
Ian Massey
4 Whin Bank
Scarborough YO12 5LE
Tel: 01723 373178

Yorkshire Tourist Board
312 Tadcaster Road
York YO24 1GS
Tel: 01904 707961
Email: info@ytb.org.uk
Website: www.ytb.org.uk

Yorkshire Wildlife Trust
10 Toft Green
York YO1 1JT
Tel: 01904 659570

NATIONAL PARK CENTRES

The Moors Centre (National Park
  Centre), Danby
Whitby YO21 2NB
Tel: 01287 660654

Sutton Bank:
National Park Centre
Sutton Bank
Thirsk YO7 2EH
Tel: 01845 597426

Old Coastguard Station (centre run
  jointly with the National Trust)
Robin Hood's Bay
Tel: 01947 880623

Aurora borealis

TOURIST INFORMATION CENTRES

Great Ayton:
High Green Car Park
Great Ayton TS9 6BJ
Tel: 01642 722835
Guisborough:
Priory Grounds
Church Street
Guisborough TS14 6QF
Tel: 01287 633801
Helmsley:
Market Place
Helmsley
York YO62 5BL
Tel: 01439 770173

Pickering:
Eastgate Car Park
Pickering YO18 0LH
Tel: 01751 473791

Whitby:
Langborne Road
Whitby YO12 1DH
Tel: 01947 602674

ATTRACTIONS

Beck Isle Museum
Bridge Street, Pickering
YO18 8DU
Tel: 01751 473653

Byland Abbey
Coxwold, York
Tel: 01347 868614

Captain Cook Schoolroom
   Museum
High Street
Great Ayton
Middlesbrough
Tel: 01642 724296

Captain Cook Memorial Museum
Grape Lane
Whitby
Tel: 01947 601900

Captain Cook & Staithes Heritage
  Centre
High Street
Staithes
Whitby
Tel: 01947 841454

Dalby Forest Drive and Visitor
  Centre
Low Dalby
Pickering
Tel: 01751 460295

The Moors Centre
Whitby
Tel: 01287 660654

Duncombe Park
Helmsley
Tel: 01439 770213

Guisborough Priory
Guisborough
TeL: 01287 633801

Guisborough Forest and Walkway
  Visitor Centre
Pinchinthorpe Station
Guisborough
Tel: 01287 6311132

Helmsley Castle
Helmsley
Tel: 01439 770442

Mount Grace Priory
Osmotherley
Northallerton
Tel: 01609 883494

North Yorkshire Moors Railway
Pickering
Tel: 01751 472508

Nunnington Hall
Nunnington
York
Tel: 01439 748283

Pickering Castle
Pickering
Tel: 01751 474989

National Trust Coastal Centre
Ravenscar
Scarborough
Tel: 01723 870138

Rievaulx Abbey
Rievaulx
Helmsley
Tel: 01439 798228

Rievaulx Terrace and Temples
Rievaulx
Helmsley
Tel: 01439 798340

Ryedale Folk Museum
Hutton-le-Hole
Tel: 01751 417367

Shandy Hall
Coxwold
York
Tel: 01347 868465

Staintondale Shire Horses
East Side Farm
Staintondale
Scarborough
Tel: 01723 870458

Whitby Abbey
Whitby
Tel: 01947 603568

Whitby Archives and Heritage
  Centre
Grape Lane
Whitby
Tel: 01947 600170
Whitby Pannet Park Museum
  & Art Gallery
Pannet Park
Whitby
Tel: 01947 602908

MAPS

The following Ordnance Survey
maps are highly recommended for
the detailed exploration of the
National Park.

Tourist Map (1:63,369)
North York Moors
Outdoor Leisure Maps (1:25,000)
No 26 North York Moors – Western
Area
No 27 North York Moors – Eastern
Area
Landranger Maps (1:50,000)
No 93: Cleveland & Darlington
No 94: Whitby
No 100: Malton & Pickering
No 101: Scarborough

FURTHER READING

Hall, A., *On Foot in the North York
  Moors* (David & Charles, 1997)
Heselden, J. and Snelling, R. (editors),
  North York Moors Leisure Guide (AA
  & OS, 1987)
Mead, H., *Inside the North York Moors*
  (Smith Settle, 1994)
North York Moors National Park
  Management Plan (North York
  Moors National Park Authority,
  1998)
Osborne, R., *The Floating Egg*
  (Pimlico, 1999)
Rhea, N., *Portrait of the North York
  Moors* (Robert Hale, 1985)
Sampson, I., *Cleveland Way* (Aurum
  Press, 1999)
Spratt, D.A. and Harrison, B.J.D. (edi-
  tors), *The North York Moors Landscape
  Heritage* (North York Moors
  National Park Authority, 1996)
Staniforth, I., *Geology of the North York
  Moors* (North York Moors National
  Park Authority, 1993)
Sykes, N., *Wild Plants and their
  Habitats in the North York Moors*
  (North York Moors National Park
  Authority, 1993)

Note: In addition to the above, a
considerable number of informative
books, booklets and leaflets are also
published by the North York Moors
National Park Authority. A list is
available on request.

Index

Page numbers in *italics* indicate illustrations